THE TEAM BUILDER

Frank R. Lewis

Dedication

This book is lovingly dedicated to the team builders who dared to see what could be. Among them are:

Robert Malsbarry	*Clelie Wilborne*
J. Walker Campbell	*Bob Norvell*
Michael Rochelle	*Brooks Faulkner*

It is also fondly dedicated to the team members I knew during my ministry at Green Valley Baptist Church, Henderson, Nevada, including:

Steve Espinosa	*Andy Peterman*
David Pohto	*Mark Terry*
Edward Moreno	*Steve Pearson*
Chris Willeke	*Phillip Williams*

ISBN 0-7673-9277-9

Dewey Decimal Classification: 254

Subject Heading: CHURCH STAFF

Printed in the United States of America

Pastor-Staff Leadership Department

The Sunday School Board of

the Southern Baptist Convention

127 Ninth Avenue, North

Nashville, Tennessee 37234

Contents

Introduction: A Vision Statement for Team Building

The headlines read, "SOFTWARE CATCHES THE TEAM SPIRIT New computer programs may soon change the way groups of people work."[1] What a concept! Having invaded the world by storm, computers have changed just about everything, even our working relationships. But, rest easy; the church is still safe from innovation.

God is gracious, and if He sends the revival that some sense is possible in the next few years, the church is going to have to make some changes in how we do business or else be voted out of business when new followers of the Way show up wondering what we've been up to for the past two thousand years of church history. Clearly, we need several changes, one of which is a major overhaul in pastoral leadership in the local churches.

Everyone is talking about vision statements these days. Businesses have them. People with good habits have them. There is a rumor that churches are writing them. A vision statement inspired this book. It is my vision to see the pastoral staff in the local churches of America replaced with pastoral teams. It is my vision to see evidence of Paul-Timothy relationships in our churches among our pastors.

For nearly 20 years I watched pastors and church leaders come and go. For the past 16 years I have been involved in professional ministry as a member of a church staff or its leader. This experience has enabled me to see the leadership team of a local church from various perspectives. Today, as a member of the Church Leadership Services Division of the Baptist Sunday School Board, I come in contact with pastor-leaders from churches of many different sizes. My vision statement grows out of these experiences and my hopes for the days ahead as the church enters into what some are calling the most promising days in all of church history.

The Team Builder is the first resource of its kind designed to assist the pastor of a local church with leading and developing the team of God-called servants gathered around him. It is a guide for building stronger personal relationships among professional ministry leaders in the local church. My friend and teammate, Ron Pratt, laughingly says that when a pastor has grown tired of leading by intimidation, he might want to try being relational. I call it "leading by grace." Hopefully we'll see it called common in days to come.

The objective of this resource is fourfold. By means of the following pages, I hope to help you *better understand the New Testament model of pastoral leadership.* If you understand this model better, I think it will enable you to *build the strongest team of pastoral leaders* you've ever known. If you succeed in building this team of pastoral leaders, you will begin to *inspire and encourage the others around you to do more for the kingdom of God* than they've ever done before.

To put it another, more blatant way, I hope to *change your vocabulary.* When you have finished reading this resource, if not before, I hope to have eradicated the term "staff" from your vocabulary with regard to those serving beside you in vocational ministry leadership positions. I hope you will begin to call them team members and, if appropriate, pastors.

The reason is simple. There needs to be a radical change in the way we relate to one another as professional church leaders. Duty demands it. Culture will, too, if God ever sends national renewal. Look at the reality of where we are in almost any denomination.

There is a rapid turnover of ministry professionals in church life today.

Being in ministry is viewed by most clergy as hazardous to their marriages and family relationships.

One of the major reasons for conflict in the church today continues to be personnel-related issues, specifically, poor working relationships with senior pastors. Unscriptural expectations of the role of the senior pastor contribute to this ungodly model. He's the only man who "works only one day a week" yet is given the most exhaustive job description in history. In some cases churches have adopted hiring policies without giving proper attention to the ministry calling and gifts of potential pastoral leaders.

Another contributing factor is the limited understanding of shared ministry between senior pastors and others in ministry leadership positions in the local church. With no understanding of a purpose statement and no specific vision for what God wants the church to accomplish, we've mastered the game of doing church via intimidation. We work hard at doing church work. We measure success as our ability to avoid church conflict. We maintain the existing models we call church staff.

The New Testament model of pastoral leadership requires one to be a team builder. This book is intended primarily for pastors who work with other professional ministers on a church staff. If the model is implemented, ownership of the ministry will be further developed, loyalty and trust will grow, ministerial integrity will begin to grow at an accelerated pace, and the congregation and community will take notice and be blessed for it.

Be warned. Taking this book seriously will require some changes in what most of us have been doing in pastoral relationships in our churches. You will find yourself stumbling over your words as you change your vocabulary and seek to educate your church. You will have to change the routine of "staff meetings" and begin planning "team meetings" instead. You may have to plan a retreat for the sole purpose of ministering to your team members and their families. You may find out that your church has more than one pastor!

What you are about to read is working in churches all over our country. Part of it is the reality of a younger generation coming of age in our churches. It may be the result of a cultural abandonment of a system that worked well in post-war America but no longer serves today's leadership standard. I'd like to think it is a coming reality in preparation for something God is going to do that is bigger and greater than any of us can imagine.

Let's build His team!

Frank R. Lewis

---

[1]Louis S. Richman, *Fortune,* vol. 115 (8 June 1987): 125.

CHAPTER 1

New Testament Patterns for Team-Building Leadership

Family members have arrived and the small apartment that has been home becomes overcrowded overnight. Excitement fills the air with a note of accomplishment and celebration. Hours later, you find your place in a distinguished line of equally excited, accomplished celebrants. The institutional registrar calls your name. You walk across a platform framed by the watchful eyes of professional academicians. With one hand you grasp a diploma; with the other you shake the hand of an institutional mentor. With the next step, you become a credentialed church leader, mentally skilled and spiritually prepared for an assault on the gates of hell. Congratulations. You are now a professional minister.

Like many who have gone on before you, your bookshelf is bulging with commentaries and countless sermons by Herschel Ford, G. Campbell Morgan, Vance Havner, and others. You have neatly filed your sermon briefs from preaching classes and now feel ready to face your first six months on the post-seminarian field. You have already loaded the rented moving van. Some of your seminarian peers not only loaded their vans, they left the engine running so as to save time following the commencement, anxious not so much to get to the new field of service as to see the seminary campus in the rear view mirror. You are now on your way to pastor your first church. Set your watch. It's time for you to prepare yourself for Christianity's number one, non-televised game show entitled, "Things They Never Taught Me in Seminary."

If that sounds critical, hear this: Seminary is not supposed to teach you everything. Nowhere else in the world can you learn systematic theology as you can in seminary. No other environment provides for you the opportunity to forge lifelong ministerial relationships. No other learning center cares about the impact that the Aorist Stem or the Qal Imperfect could have on the human heart. Seminary is a great place. I have studied in three of them and would be there now if God's call permitted it. Almost every pastor finds himself one day coming to the conclusion that there is something lacking in his training. Pastors often express this in terms lamenting a seminarian proficiency, but the reality is that some things are not taught there.

Behold, leadership. Traveling at altitudes of 2,500 feet, you can learn more from an in-flight magazine on the subject of leadership than is taught in most master's level seminary classrooms. In the center section of these wonderful textbooks of the sky, one can read the following quotes almost daily:

> TEAMWORK: There is no limit to what you can accomplish if it does not matter who gets the credit.
>
> TEAMWORK: Working together means winning together.
>
> TEAMWORK: Coming together is a beginning. Keeping together is progress. Working together is success.
>
> TRUST: When a gifted team dedicates itself to unselfish trust and combines instinct with boldness and effort—it is ready to climb.

Like proverbs from the pen of Solomon, these pregnant expressions bulge with practical insight and ring with such truth that most would call them inspired, yea, even inerrant. Framed against a backdrop of world-class athletes or the incomparable beauty of nature scenes, each proverb could be yours to display with pride in your office. With the plethora of CEO mentalities occupying pastors' studies these days, such decorum could be fitting. I trust you are reading this book because you want more than a stylish office; you want an influential ministry. As John Maxwell has said many times, "Leadership is influence." What does God's Word say about leadership?

New Testament Patterns for Church Leadership

As the New Testament church began to grow in the midst of a hostile first-century environment, church-leadership patterns began to appear. The office of the deacon emerged as a solution to a pastoral-care need in the fast growing congregation in Jerusalem. The apostles recognized the importance of devoting their time and attention to prayer and the Word of God.

The seven individuals selected to perform the ministry of servants evidently performed their tasks so well, that they served as a model for other congregations (see Rom. 16:1; Phil. 1:1).

Look again at the plural noun used to describe the leadership of the Jerusalem church in Acts 6. They are refereed to as "the twelve" and "the apostles." In other words, nurturing the incredible growth of the church was the experience base of multiple spiritual leaders, each devoted to prayer and the study of God's Word. No wonder the Acts account is so dramatic!

Strictly speaking, the office of apostle was for a limited time, based on the definition of the word itself. A qualification of an apostle in the strictest sense was to be an eyewitness to the earthly ministry of Jesus. Those who claim to be apostles today will not appreciate this, but the definition is a scriptural one. The modern-day function of this office may be that of a church planter, one who travels from point to point for the purpose of establishing new churches. There is a popular view that elders are the only essential leaders carried over from the old dispensation of the Old Testament to the new dispensation of the New Testament church. Etymologically, *elder* is a generic term indicating one who has maturity both physically and mentally. (See the first elders in the Mosaic administration, Deut. 1:13–15.) Generically, a Christian elder is one who has maturity and a wealth of godly experience forged in a lifestyle of discipleship. In the New Testament passages the term *elder* is interchangeable with the terms that are indicative of the role of the pastor. One Bible dictionary states it this way: "The 'elders' of the New Testament church were the 'pastors' (Eph. 4:11), 'bishops or overseers' (Acts 20:28), 'leaders' and 'rulers' (Heb. 13:7; 1 Thess. 5:12) of the flock. Everywhere in the New Testament bishop and presbyter are titles given to one and the same officer of the Christian church."[1]

While most pastors will look with respect to the older (elder) members of the body for their spiritual maturity and Christian experience, the term *ruling elders* is simply another way of describing the role of pastoral leadership in the New Testament church. Paul wrote Titus and instructed him to appoint elders in the congregations of Crete. It only makes sense that these elders were the pastors. Can you imagine Paul sending Titus into a congregation that already had a pastor to appoint a ruling body for the congregation? It does not make sense.

Many congregations today utilize a third office to perform all of the administrative responsibilities of the congregation and to be a prayer and support group around the pastor. In many of these congregations, the term *elder* describes this office. The New Testament uses the word *elder* to describe the ministry function, not the office. There are passages in the New Testament that may arguably support a third office. On the other hand, function, not office seems to be the consistent emphasis. When Jethro, a man who obviously understood the shepherd/sheep motif, introduced the idea to Moses, function was crucial, not office. Having a group of skilled, loyal, proven church leaders to handle the administrative details of the church and the sensitive issues surrounding the pastor is fine. Ordaining such individuals or recognizing them with a scriptural office seems unnecessary, if not un-biblical.

Peter addresses a plural body of elders in 1 Peter 5:1–4. What he gives them is a definite description of the pastoral ministry, not a lay office of church administrators.

> *The elders which are among you I exhort, who am also an elder, and a witness of the sufferings of Christ, and also a partaker of the glory that shall be revealed: Feed the flock of God which is among you, taking the oversight thereof, not by constraint, but willingly; not for filthy lucre, but of a ready mind; neither as being lords over God's heritage, but being ensamples to the flock. And when the chief Shepherd shall appear, ye shall receive a crown of glory that fadeth not away.*

Notice that there are multiple spiritual leaders in this passage. The letter was probably intended for multiple congregations. As the letter circulates, elders (pastors) in each congregation are challenged to be faithful in their ministry of the word and in leading the church by personal example. There are no assistant elders, assistant pastors, nor staff. Similarly there is no mention in this passage nor elsewhere in the New Testament of the words "senior pastor." The closest term to this is "chief Shepherd," which is an obvious reference to Jesus Christ (1 Pet. 5:4).

Because of the rapid spread of the gospel in the first century, the financial impact of Roman persecution, and the cultural realities into which Christianity was born, the New Testament church most certainly did not have the luxury of what we know today as multiple staffing. It is difficult to imagine a pastor, minister of education, youth minister, and secretary in the first-century church. However, the evidence is strong that in each local congregation, multiple ministry gifts existed.

And he gave some, apostles; and some, prophets; and some, evangelists; and some, pastors and teachers. (Eph. 4:11)

The emergence of distinctive ministry vocations is relatively new. However, the gifts date back to the Jerusalem church and the coming of the Holy Spirit. Somehow in the past 2,000 years of church history, we have come to recognize some ministry gifts as more important than others. Even though we preach sermons that say we do not, our leadership patterns betray us.

The Validity of the Pastoral Team

Pastors equip our churches today, as they did the churches of Paul and Peter's day. Some of these pastors have the spiritual gifts and calling to be preachers. Some have the gifts and calling to be pastors using their gifts and talents in music and drama as the arena for their ministry. Some pastors have a calling to pastor our youth or single adults. Others have the gift of teaching and administration and are pastors serving in the area of religious education. In some congregations, there are multiple "preaching pastors." Other congregations have pastors who give special attention to the needs of the homeless, the hospitalized, the institutionalized, the confused, the abused, the newest converts, and newly married. The list seems endless. All are called. All are gifted spiritually, some with skills and talents that exceed others. All are ministers, not necessarily by profession, for some hold other work responsibilities in order to minister in some places. This book is a call to recognize each in their own right as *a pastor—one called out with a message, sent by God, leading the flock of God, under the biblical authority established in Scripture, a member of a body, an integral part of a functional team.*

By consensus of the body, the pastor who has the responsibility for preaching is usually the leader responsible for the other pastors who may serve the congregation. In this case, the staff (a term we will visit in chapter 3) is supervised by the pastor. Hebrews 13 mentions the pastor's authority over the congregation and, subsequently, the members of the pastoral team (staff). "Team building" pastors have earned the right to be leaders. Regardless of the circumstances, they either inherit a team of called, skilled, gifted individuals and earn the right to lead them, or they start from scratch, enable a congregation to dream about the future, and build their team carefully toward the realization of that dream.

The translated biblical terms which describe the functions of the office of pastor are *episkopos*—bishop or overseer, *presbuteros*—elder, *poimen*—shepherd, and *angelos*—messengers. Dr. Mike Miller uses the terms *leading, administering, ministering,* and *communicating* to describe these functional terms in their biblical context.[2] The role of Kingdom leader in our churches finds its natural expression in the dedicated shepherd-leader-communicator we call pastor. The deacons, by function, serve the Lord by serving the congregation as an extension of the pastoral-care ministry of the pastoral team (see Acts 6). By function, deacons do not comprise a board. They are not the ruling elders of the church, unless it is a dysfunctional church. They lead by example and function, not by office. They lead under the authority of the pastor, or they mislead.

The ideal pastoral team encompasses the professional and lay ministers of the body of believers, that is, pastors, deacons, and laity. Each serves in the sphere of freedom, recognizing the biblical pattern of authority given them to exercise their spiritual gifts.

Building a pastoral team is basic to the New Testament recognition of spiritual gifts and the growth of a healthy church body. No individual pastor possesses all of the gifts nor the time and energy required to meet every need in every congregation effectively. Only the spiritually gifted individuals of a congregation can do this. As the body grows, a pastoral team can motivate members more effectively if the process of team building is mastered.

Team building begins with the fundamental skills of genuine leadership. The high profile that is often given to the preaching pastor might seem to be the basis for making him the team leader. In reality, it is the spiritual capacity to be a leader that enables him to fulfill this role of team builder. Pretenders lead from a shallow skill base and a platform of positional leadership. Thankfully, they often only lead for a short period of time; but, sadly, inestimable damage is often done during their tenures. Team builders lead by example, displaying a servant's attitude and a coach's concern. Team-building pastors understand accountability and responsibility as spiritual realities. The scriptural admonitions for these are abundant. Perhaps none is so stern as that found in Acts where Paul addresses the Ephesian elders (plural) of the church in Ephesus (singular):

Take heed therefore unto yourselves, and to all the flock, over the which the Holy Ghost hath made you overseers, to feed the church of God, which he hath purchased with his own blood. (Acts 20:28)

We are leaders and administrators. The team-building pastor senses not only the urgency of this call, but also the challenge of leading others to respond to the call in ways that impact the church for years to come.

Think of sports teams that have won successive titles in their fields. Commentators use terms like *dynasty* to describe them. Their coaches are generally held in high esteem for building a united, goal-oriented, focused team. Yet none of these sports teams shares the distinction that belongs to the church; none of them are blood bought. Team-building pastors build dynasties, teams that win, teams that accomplish tremendous things to the glory of God because they understand something about the team's ownership. Unlike professional sports teams, the ownership is not fickle, nor driven by press releases, nor subject to economic pressures. As we begin to remember the price paid by the Owner, a price paid in blood, we find the motivation to do our best as instruments of the Owner.

Enter the Team Builder from Nazareth. Since we are talking about team-building leadership in the church, Jesus becomes our consummate model. Come see the familiar with new lenses. The observations are quite simple. Their impact is unlimited.

The Consummate Team-Building Model: Servant Leadership

Jesus built a team with twelve players. None were all-stars. None brought experience to the mission. Yet, through all but one of them, the world was turned upside-down. Jesus used no tests nor psychological instruments upon which to base their selection, and no head-hunter firm to find them. He placed no want ads in the *Pharisaic Journal*. Instead, He invited men to follow him, He prayed, and then He made His selection (see Matt. 4:18—5:1, Mark 3:13–19). Throughout this three-year ministry these men watched and learned much from Jesus. At times we see them showing little evidence of faith, and at other times we see immaturity.

In putting together a great team, it is important to have appropriate expectations of the team members. Jesus exemplifies this. His expectations were always appropriate in that He gave clear directions and challenged the men to do something that was slightly beyond their natural ability. Notice the reaction of the twelve when they returned from being sent out for their first mission tour. They saw things they never dreamed they would see. They experienced victory. The follow-up meeting with Jesus was a time of celebration.

When the mother of two team members came to negotiate a contract with Jesus related to future seating arrangements in the Kingdom, Jesus used the opportunity to teach a spiritual truth about greatness in God's eyes. His reaction was one of grace. In too many places today, alienation, if not termination, would mark a positional leader's response.

The final lesson unfolds in the upper room on the night of Jesus' arrest. The dinner conversation had turned to reflection as the Passover meal was being remembered. This somber time of ritual worship, rich and meaningful, preoccupied the thoughts of each person in the room. Jesus stood, removed the upper portion of His robe, took the servant's towel and the wash basin. While the basin had been in the room all evening, it was comfortably distanced from the reach of those gathered for the meal. Without fanfare, almost without notice, Jesus began washing the feet of the disciples.

Imagine the scene. For days tension has been building, but for now it is easier for the disciples to pretend all is well. As Jesus emerges from the shadow-draped corners of that upper room, He does so without so much as clearing His throat. Even the first disciple approached does not realize what is taking place. Quickly he moves his foot, thinking Jesus is trying to get something. As his foot is held tightly in the grip of the leader, he is disarmed by the look in Jesus' eyes. The grip softens to a tender embrace, and as it does, the volume in the room begins to decrease. Stories of past remembrances fade, and by the time Jesus approaches the second set of feet, the room is uncharacteristically quiet.

Listen to the sounds in the nearly silent room. The first sound is that of water running off the feet of a spellbound and surprised disciple. Not a word breaks the room's silence, though volumes are recorded upon each heart. Somewhere between the sound of Jesus' knees cracking as He bends before a new set of dust-pocked feet and the wringing of the servant's towel in the wash basin, one disciple slips away into the night, unnoticed by the others. For him, this display of servanthood only affirms an earlier decision to sabotage. Yet, the lesson in leadership goes deep into the hearts of those remaining.

If you could hear the echo in the heart as Jesus gently washes a new pair of feet, you would hear the serendipitous realization that *true leadership springs from servanthood.* Though it took the eleven men days to assimilate this truth, it was already being written upon the inner heart.

What Happened When He Washed Feet

The model for leadership, in what would become His last teaching moment during His physical life on earth, imparted one of the greatest lessons on leadership ever observed. First, Jesus stepped out completely from the spotlight, or the platform of positional leadership. There were countless reasons why someone else should have taken the initiative if not the assignment to take up the servant's bowl. Still, it is Jesus who carries it. The positional leader is never willing to vacate his place of authority for fear that he will never get it back. Jesus already knew how to do this. Years later, the early church might sing this truth as a hymn. But on this night, before twelve sets of eyes and feet, Jesus demonstrated clearly that He . . .

> *Being in the form of God, thought it not robbery to be equal with God: But made himself of no reputation, and took upon him the form of a servant, and was made in the likeness of men: And being found in fashion as a man, he humbled himself, and became obedient unto death, even the death of the cross. Wherefore God also hath highly exalted him, and given him a name which is above every name: That at the name of Jesus every knee should bow, of things in heaven, and things in earth, and things under the earth; And that every tongue should confess that Jesus Christ is Lord, to the glory of God the Father. (Phil. 2:6–11)*

Jesus dispelled before the eyes of those closest to Him, the notion that He led out of position or privilege. He stepped out of the seat of honor that was His at the Passover table, shed the outer garment that served to give him what little dignity might be His as a renegade rabbi, and wrapped a servant's towel around His waist. The disciples had never seen anything like it before. Jesus was already used to it.

Today's team-building pastor already will have come to the place in his heart where he is *willing to risk position and privilege,* and step into *a role of vulnerability.* Then, those closest to him will be touched, ministered to, instructed with word pictures that are undeniably clear, and prepared to do likewise when the pressure of leadership falls to their shoulders.

The second thing done by Jesus is so simple we often overlook it. You cannot wash feet unless you are willing to touch feet. Jesus touched every member of His team. He touched them in a place that most in our world would rather not touch. He touched their feet. Tender. Callused in spots. Dirty from the dusty streets upon which they walked. Tired from the days journey that brought them to this seminar on leadership. Feet that had followed. Feet that would soon scatter. Feet that never knew the comfort of a Rockport®, nor the advantage of a Nike. Feet that were plain, yet beautiful. Feet that had carried good news in the past. Feet that would do so again in the days ahead.

Team-builders know the importance of the appropriate touch. The touch of friendship and the touch of ministry are two touches that team members need. One says, "I am in this with you," and the other says, "I am in this for you." It is a touch of concern and a touch of encouragement. It is a touch that goes to the vulnerable and unlovely spots of every team member and assures them with little if anything spoken, that they are loved and valued.

Jesus washed His disciples' feet, and the team builder has to provide a redemptive place for ministry even to his team members. There are going to be mistakes unless your team members are not human. In some cases there will be failure. Washing the feet and touching the team will not prevent failure, but it will provide the environment to deal with failures and mistakes redemptively.

Another thing Jesus taught the disciples that night was "you never lose when you wash feet." Team builders who learn this lesson early in ministry are saved from volumes of words that once said, can never be erased. Jesus would have been powerfully capable in telling Peter the enormous grief he would have over his forthcoming denials. Jesus could have issued stern warnings about sleeping when His followers should have been praying if not at least standing guard. He could have yelled to get their attention and displayed time charts and unraveled ancient prophecy, but instead, He washed feet.

My college Hebrew professor often said, "Being right is such a little thing." There are countless times when senior supervisors understand far more than their younger, less experienced supervisees. There are other times when a church antagonist will make life miserable for the pastor-leader. At times like this, being right may be a little thing. The kingdom of God will be better served by washing feet. *We'll never lose, especially in God's eyes, when we wash feet.*

Finally, Jesus led the disciples to the garden when the lessons from the upper room had been presented. The lessons were not yet complete, for the disciples had to unpack their meaning in the course of the days ahead. But Jesus still had influence. He was still in control. The team, bound by a sense of loyalty that was beyond their ability to comprehend, followed Him to a familiar place of prayer. They followed with clean feet and much more.

The team-builder washes feet every chance he gets. Sometimes it is in the servant-motivated things we do for those who serve along side of us. We remember them on special days; we include them in special events. Other times we surprise them by cutting their grass when they vacation during the summer. We insist that they take a day off when a spouse has a holiday. We drop in their office and close the door just to laugh or cry, and sometimes pray with them, spontaneously.

Team-builders never lose when they wash feet.

---

[1] *Eaton's Bible Dictionary.*

[2] Michael D. Miller, *Kingdom Leadership: A Call to Christ-Centered Leadership* (Nashville: Convention Press, 1996), 67.

INTERACTIVE APPLICATION

What words would you use to describe your leadership style?

What words do you think those who serve alongside you would use to describe your leadership style? Why do you feel this way?

What did you do the last time you exemplified servant leadership?

What is inconsistent in your life today, preventing you from being a servant leader?

CHAPTER 2

The Single-Member Pastoral Team

The biggest frustration felt by the pastor of the single staff church is trying to get all the essential things done week after week, all by yourself. There is a sense of loneliness and isolation because there is no one else in a paid ministry position with which to plan and dream. The feeling of riding the tubular wave like a single surfer best describes the experience. The pastor is the surfer. The wave represents everything that needs to be done in the church, and it is about to roll over you. The surfboard may well represent the church. Learning to ride the wave well determines how one will navigate the single-staff church.

There obviously are some important things to do if you lead one of the 25,000 single-member pastoral team churches today. I love the quote often shared in conferences for single-staff pastors, "I'm presently pastoring a single-staff church, but I don't plan for it to be a single-staff church very long." This is a statement of faith and vision. God's faithfulness proves it to be true. Let's examine the basics.

Basics for Balance

With so many things to do, what does the pastor of a single-member pastoral team do first? The surprising answer is not that different from what the pastor of a multimember pastoral team church needs to do. You have to major on the things that matter most. It's that simple. The difficult thing is that majoring on the things that matter most may require more discipline in the single-member pastoral team church, because there is a sense that less accountability is involved. It is easier to put off the difficult decisions and the difficult disciplines when there is no one around to watch. If left unguarded, complacency can saturate the study, and hopelessness can overwhelm the spirit. Because of this, the pastor of the single-member pastoral team church must exercise extreme caution and give dedicated attention to the basics.

There are three basics. Without mastering them you will attempt ministry in a frustrating and barren environment. **Establish the disciplines that will sustain you, cultivate the relationships that will nurture you, and develop a vision that is going to motivate and protect you.** There will be several other urgencies throughout your ministry. Determining that the three basics will never yield to the multiple urgencies that seek to distract you will distinguish the ministry God is blessing from those He is not.

Establish Disciplines That Will Sustain You

Daily Private Worship

The primary discipline for balance for the pastor of the single-member pastoral team (single staff) church is to listen for a fresh word from God every day. The first discipline of the pastor-leader must be that of a *daily private worship experience involving prayer and the Word of God.* The pastor of the single-member pastoral team church is going to discover enough interruptions, enough urgent requests, enough genuine and needful responsibilities, to relegate the discipline of "quiet time" to the back burner of his life indefinitely. Make no mistake about it, Satan loves to keep it this way.

The early years of ministry were busy years. Looking back on them, especially from the vantage point of having pastored my first church for10 years and seeing it grow significantly, I can honestly tell any pastor that the early years will provide a foundation for every year to come. You will establish the study habits, visitation patterns, leadership ethic, and devotional patterns that will characterize your ministry for decades. Though you probably do not want to hear this, it is true that as your church grows and adds other professional ministers to the team, your work load is going to increase. In other words, it will never be easier for you to become spiritually disciplined than right now!

So let me ask the hard question to every pastor, those who serve alone as the professional minister of a local church, and those who have a multiple-minister team surrounding them. Will your present devotional patterns carry you forward along the leadership path, or will they hinder you in the journey as a spiritual leader? Here is another way of asking this same question in an even more pointed fashion: "Will your next staff addition have to backslide spiritually in order to experience the depth of your spiritual disciplines?"

The single most important thing the pastor of a church can do is cultivate within him the unmistakable image of Jesus Christ. This will not happen without a disciplined determination to nurture the spirit through intimate fellowship with Christ. Because this is true regardless of the size of the church, every pastor must embrace its importance. What you do next really won't matter unless first you honestly see yourself as a growing and developing disciple of Jesus Christ.

How are you going to do this? There are many methods today by which men and women practice the spiritual disciplines. Some read through a book of the Bible. Others read devotional literature and great Christian classics. Some spend hours in prayer. Some even fast. My way is not any more or less spiritual than the others, but what I want to share with pastors is a tested and proven discipline that really works. I know this because I have practiced it for 18 years. The problem with many disciplines is that they never become habits. I'm careful not to worship the habit, but the habit inevitably helps me worship.

Journaling

With the exception of the Holy Spirit of God, I cannot think of any one single thing that has had more "keeping" power in my life than journaling. I began journaling in college after hearing Milt Hughes introduce the *Spiritual Journey Notebook* to a group of BSU students at a Summer Missions retreat. What he shared absolutely changed my life. I had been a Christian for eight years at the time and had faithfully read my Bible on a near daily basis. I spent time in prayer almost every day. Usually these things were done at night prior to going to bed. It was not uncommon for me to drift to sleep during the prayer time. Somewhat innocently, I convinced myself that since there were worse things one could do while drifting to sleep, this must be all right.

Milt Hughes challenged me to get up early in the morning to begin my day with prayer and a devotional Bible reading. Then he challenged me to journal my thoughts, impressions, prayers, or questions as a part of the devotional time. I began by setting my alarm clock five minutes earlier than usual. This was not long enough by the end of the first week. Soon, this changed to 15 minutes and eventually became half an hour. For a college student to make this change, the activity has to be valuable. I found great value in the realization that God wanted to speak to me through His word. I also discovered that my mind and heart were much more sensitive to His voice in the early hours than in the late evening hours. My journal notes occupied the space of only a small paragraph in the beginning, but a year or two later, I found myself reading the journal entries, and I discovered a great confirmation of the work of God in my life re-reading the entries I had made earlier. Visiting those journal entries made 12 months earlier was like pausing at spiritual mile markers or scenic stops along the path of my spiritual journey. It encouraged a deeper and more intentional discipline knowing that today's entry might become tomorrow's reaffirmation during difficult, unforeseen times.

I carried this discipline with me in seminary. In my first church, I confess, I somehow got terribly sidetracked from this and other disciplines. The evidence is clear. I stepped out of God's will for my life at the time, and the last thing I was going to do was keep a journal of the day-to-day mistakes. Unfortunately the mistakes grew worse before the conviction and repentance took place. Again looking back, it is like a survey of a mountain scene. I could see the high points in my life and observe through the journal how they were underscored with a growing, daily worship experience. When my private worship was consistent, the life was fruitful. Conversely, when the discipline was neglected, my life became like a cesspool.

Speaking of accountability, I challenge you to find a more telling, revealing accountability partner than a journal. Blank pages never lie. Full ones never have to be read. When they are, the discipline is encouraged with confirmations too deep for words.

If I could tell a pastor one thing to do that would affect his ministry more than anything else, it would be to *take the matter of personal spiritual growth more seriously than anything else in life.* The man who begins his day with God is going to be different because of it in the long run.

Journaling is a discipline. Its effects are incredible when measured over the long haul. I genuinely believe there is a therapeutic benefit that God gives us when we learn early in life to cast all our cares upon Him. The stress found in the ministry is life threatening. Journaling enables a person to have a natural outlet for daily stress. But it is much more than that. In this time of "spilling out" to God, God ministers to the spirit, soul, and body of the man. No human counselor is capable of duplicating this kind of inner ministry.

The satisfaction that comes from looking at a tangible reminder of a thing accomplished is a rare feeling in the professional minister's life. There is always something else that could have been done in the average week of the minister's life. When Sunday morning rolls around with its rhythmic regularity, we lament that we could have made more visits, we could have discovered clearer illustrations, we could have performed deeper word studies. However, when a pastor knows that he has been faithful in matters pertaining to his own spiritual growth, there is a sense of godly confidence that saturates the rest of the week's responsibilities and positions the man to trust God in ways that he has not experienced before.

Taken one step further, journaling enables us to be more effective as communicators of divine truth. One of the most life impacting books I ever read was *Too Busy Not To Pray* by Bill Hybles. I read this book long after I had cultivated the discipline of journaling. It took me one giant step further. Bill Hybles addresses an area where many of us struggle in our prayer life when he speaks about wandering minds. Frustration was a constant companion following my quiet time because I found myself thinking about issues totally unrelated to my devotion or my prayer requests when I was supposed to be praying. I'd begin all right, but soon I would be thinking about everything under the sun. Things I would never pray about would fill my mind during this "audience with God" time. How embarrassing! How humbling. (As if I needed another reminder of my sinful nature.) Maybe I suffered from a latent form of Attention Deficit -Hyperactivity Disorder, but I could not seem to focus my attention on praying to save my life. When I discovered the *discipline of writing out my prayers to God,* everything changed.

This impacted the intimacy curve of my devotional life more than anything I had ever imagined. I discovered the discipline of praying without using the first person pronoun "I" during the praise time of the prayer. Confession of sin became a much more serious moment as I had to not only recall sin, but write it out and look at it in black and white. Writing my prayers enabled me to become more sensitive to the provision of God as I thanked Him for the blessings in life. Writing the requests that were on my heart moved me to pray in ways that I had never prayed before as I wrote the names of family members, church members, lost people, missionaries, political figures, and dealt with other cultural or ethical issues.

Writing my prayers effected another change in my prayer life by stripping away many of the "vain repetitions" that marked my prayers. While we try to avoid the "auto-pilot" prayer language, it is difficult not to get caught up in using trite and redundant phrases. The discipline of writing our prayers will help correct this inbred habit quickly. The result is worthwhile. It has been said that a preacher can preach only as good as he can pray. When prayer becomes an accomplished discipline, you will find yourself preaching more passionately, thus effectively. Furthermore, as a worship leader you will discover that your ability to pray in ways that move the congregation in true worship, not emotion, is markedly enhanced.

It grows out of a cultivated discipline. The impact of the ministry grows because the ministry of prayer becomes real, and the discipline of cultivating the person of Jesus Christ becomes clearly evident. Nothing else in the world will impact the ministry like the effect of this one discipline. If you are practicing the disciplines, don't stop. If you are struggling, try what I've suggested. If you've never given the discipline a try and you don't intend to, please get out of the ministry and do something else with your life.

Cultivate Relationships That Will Nurture You

Ministry can be a lonely place. In the single-member pastoral team church, this loneliness can be devastating. *It becomes imperative that the pastor cultivate some relationships that will enable him to be challenged, sharpened, motivated, and affirmed.* For this reason, the pastor of the single-member pastoral team church needs to give attention to the *networks of other professional ministers* around him, or create these networks.

We were created for fellowship. I've never been called to a church where I could not experience genuine fellowship with the members in the congregation. My accountability partners were trusted laymen in the church. My wife and I enjoyed social outings with members of the congregation. Still, there was a need for a professional relationship that challenged and stretched me, even in the early years of my ministry following seminary. Ideally, what is often called the "staff meeting" in most churches should be one of the vehicles that provides such stretching. It is not always the case. As I began pastoring the mission church, I did not have a staff meeting to attend.

I did make it a point to meet other ministers in the community. These were people who were in the same vocational boat in which I found myself paddling. We were all new to a fast growing city. Most of us were pastoring our first congregations following seminary. We were all trying to survive as church starters. These commonalties, along with a naive assumption that we were all reading from the same theological pages, made our fellowship possible, and for many years, very meaningful. There was a sense of competition, but it was minor. We soon learned to celebrate one another's victories. When one congregation purchased land, it provided hope to the others that land acquisition was not impossible. When one church began growing, it encouraged the rest to pray and work hard, trusting God for growth as well.

Occasionally, this informal group of clergy attempted community projects and organized special worship events involving the participation of our respective congregations. Some of those events were very special. Over the years each church grew, purchased land, built buildings, and began to see the face of the community change with a church on nearly every major intersection. It became more difficult and less important for us to meet as often, but the professional relationships established years earlier grew into valuable ministering relationships for the future. When news of my resignation was announced, one of the pastors called to wish his best, then prayed for me over the phone. I was longing for this kind of prayer support. My copastors could not offer it at the time as they were dealing with many new feelings and emotions. I understood that. The phone call and the time of prayer was valuable to me and made me thankful for the investment I had made 10 years earlier.

One of the most valuable investments you may make in your present ministry setting is that of building a bridge with the local pastor of another church in your community. Ministerial associations can help, but informal friendships, selectively made and carefully cultivated will be more apt to minister mutually.

This also can be done through the denominational structure in most churches. There probably are other pastors of churches in your area working cooperatively through denominational affiliations such as associations, districts, fellowships, or conventions. Your involvement in the informal fellowships provided through these affiliations as well as your involvement in the formal training, continuing education, mission projects, and administrative responsibilities will put you in contact with professional ministry issues that will strengthen what you do in the local church.

As a church planter, the prayer support and encouragement I received through these relationships undoubtedly played a role in my personal and professional growth as a minister. The constant attention given to a world view of ministry enabled me to be more balanced in my approach to ministry in the local church. Involvement in this arena of ministry stretched my interpersonal relationship skills, enabling me to meet some of the most godly men I've ever met. Many of these men were old enough to be my grandfather. They were men who had seen trends in churches come and go. They were men who "stayed by the stuff" with credible track records of ministerial integrity. These relationships enriched my life. Pastors of single-member pastoral team churches will do well to cultivate these relationships.

Peer relationships among other pastors who share similar life experiences also will be a blessing. By cultivating relationships made at conference centers, state convention meetings, and continuing education settings, you will build important prayer and support networks that will enhance your ministry and encourage pastoral character. A pastor's wife will be an asset in making these relationships. She is hungry for them, and it is a natural, instinctive ability which God's grace has imparted to ministers' wives. If you doubt what I'm saying, watch how easily the wives of ministers move about in the conference centers each summer. While their professionally intensive minister-husbands navigate the terrain with clerical caution, the women are networking and looking for others with whom they can bare their souls. Some of our strongest friendships have been birthed by following the lead of my wife in these unique environments.

Develop a Vision That Will Motivate and Protect You

God's word reminds us "Where there is no vision, the people are unrestrained" (Prov. 29:18). Other translations read "Where there is no vision, the people perish." When it comes to the ministry in the local church, I paraphrase it this way, "Without a plan, frustration will drain the joy out of your ministry." The single-member pastoral team cannot do everything in the church that needs to be done. Trying to will result in frustration for everyone involved.

What kind of ministry do you think God wants you to have? Gene Mims has set forth the standard in *Kingdom Principles Growth Strategies* (Nashville: Convention Press). The process model of Kingdom Principles helps a church establish a purpose statement and a set of vision statements enabling a church to prioritize ministry. Thumbnailed, the process begins with a pastor's personal study of the Great Commission and involves a spiritual gift inventory, a community survey, and the establishment of ministry priorities. While this concept seems so obvious, it is astounding to know how many pastors and churches today are trying to do Kingdom business without a clue as to who and what they are.

A pastor's vision will include a conviction about his call, a commitment to the development and use of his spiritual gifts, and an intentional resistance to those things that would serve as distractions to faithful ministry. Learning to do this requires vision: *the ability to see beyond the present, and the persistence to settle for nothing less.* The vision motivates and protects. The vision motivates the pastor to develop his competencies in spite of difficulties. The vision protects by enabling the minister to be selective and even shielded from anything that would distract from the primary understanding of his call.

Translating this to the local church, the meaning and application is simple. Y*ou have to build a team. You must find others willing to share the vision with you, and you must enable them to partner with you in the work.* If you do not have this kind of team-building vision which multiplies your ministry, your vision is too small.

We've all heard the acrostic for TEAM "Together, Everyone Accomplishes More." The adage has been around for years. It appears in popular books with recent publication dates. I first learned it from a scoutmaster over 20 years ago. The concept is simple but true. This acrostic is an inspirational way to think of the word "team" and its significance. In the church with only one professional minister, the ministry will be multiplied only if the lay-ministers in the congregation will assist in meeting the many demands of ministry by joining the team.

Pastoral Enlistment and Empowerment List

How does a pastor begin building his team? More and more people are talking about creating a special "task" list and working from it. I'll call this the "pastoral enlistment and empowerment list." Prayerfully find the time to formulate a list of everything that you are doing as a pastor. Write everything you can think of on your list. Included on your list could be any number of the following tasks:

preaching
visiting the hospitals

evangelistic/outreach visitation
writing letters
building maintenance
premarital counseling
conducting wedding rehearsals
setting up and/or taking down meeting rooms
preparing children's sermons
enlisting workers for special needs
folding bulletins
providing transportation to and from church activities
mowing the church lawn
giving devotions at the local nursing home or jail
teaching a Sunday School class
designing and mailing the church newsletter

Everything on this list is important to some degree in the life of a church. Regardless of the size of your church, not everything is a requirement, nor should it be, of the pastor of the church. Some of these activities become inherited by pastors when they move to a local church because the previous pastor did them. That does not mean you need to continue doing them. Either the people had unrealistic expectations of their pastor, or the former pastor was doing too many things.

Prayerfully, ask God to lead you to three things on this list that you really need to be doing to be faithful as the leader God has called you to be in your church. Ask God to show you someone in the church who would do one or more of the tasks on your list if enlisted and enabled.

Enlist and Enable

"Enlisting" means that you have invited this person to share in the vision God has given you as the pastor. We make a mistake by enlisting people to tasks or programs. We succeed when we enlist people to a vision. *"Enabling" is giving an individual the training necessary and the permission needed* (sometimes this will be formal permission via church approval) *to carry out a specific responsibility.* Once you have enlisted and enabled that individual to carry out the responsibility, *mark the task off of your list.*

Continue this process until your tasks have been reduced to the three most important ones on the list. Once you have arrived at these three things, go after them with a passion. They need to drive your list of daily priorities and impact all of your future planning. You will be a better preacher/pastor for it. While some may accuse you of laziness, most will sense a renewed enthusiasm for the work you are doing. Your proficiency will improve in the areas that remain on your list, in addition, you will be building a team of lay ministers around you.

Pastoring a growing church with a large students and singles ministry put me into the arena of ministering to people who were often getting married. This is a joy-filled part of ministry in most cases. I found it fun to sit across the table with young people who were about to enter one of life's most exciting transitional times. However, I soon found myself spending several nights a week in my office with these couples completing their premarital counseling requirements. Making matters more difficult for my family was the fact that in a given month, I might be involved in several weekend weddings. This required my time on Friday nights for a rehearsal and again on Saturday for the ceremony.

To emphasize the importance of the pastoral enlistment and empowerment list, consider the hours of involvement "spent" in one wedding, multiplied by the number of weddings you probably will do in the coming year. In preparing for and conducting the premarital counseling sessions, you will spend at least six hours per couple. Regardless of your skill and intention, at least three hours will be required on Friday night to rehearse a 20-minute ceremony. Then comes "the main event" which will require a minimum of five hours on Saturday to handle everything that has to be done at the church to make the "perfect wedding" happen without a glitch. This includes opening the building for the florists and the people who want to decorate the church. You have to be there so that the bridal party can enter the building and begin taking photographs two hours before the service. There will be the chitchatting with all the family members, patrolling the building to enforce the no-smoking policy of the church, and the inevitable assistance required in finding staple guns, tape, scissors and whatever else is needed to repair broken candles or boutonniere stems. When it is time for the service to begin, you find yourself and two hundred wedding guests waiting for Uncle Seymore who is supposed to video the wedding but is lost somewhere between the hotel and your church. Finally you have to stay around to sweep all the birdseed, replace all the teaching pictures in the fellowship hall that the decorators removed in their decorating frenzy, call a taxi for the out-of-town cousins whose car is now broken down in your church parking lot, and scrape candle wax off of the commemorative Communion Table before the chairman of deacons (who gave it in memory of his dearly departed mother) sees the damage done first thing Sunday morning. Don't forget that tomorrow is Sunday, your most important day of the week. After a steady diet of weddings where you do everything yourself, you will drag your body, along with the notes required to get through the unfinished sermon, into the pulpit and "punt!"

By my count, a minister will dedicate between 14 and 20 hours for every wedding he performs. In the first years of my ministry I probably was involved in six weddings. The last year I pastored a church, I performed 20. The minimal amount of time for me was 6 weddings multiplied by 14 hours, for a total of 84 hours. This equates to two 40-hour weeks in a given year. While ministering to people in this transitional time of life is significant and worthy, I do not think it merits the equivalent of two weeks of my year as a pastor. *Behold— a more excellent way!*

I found a detail person who was willing to become the church wedding coordinator. She observed one of my wedding weekends, drew up a list of requirements, helped develop our church wedding policy, and became my right hand for all future events involving weddings. After *enlisting and enabling* this person for this task, my involvement in weddings was reduced to 45 minutes. I literally showed up at the church 15 minutes prior to the ceremony, conducted the event, signed the license, posed for one photograph with the couple, (which my coordinator arranged to be the first photo taken following the ceremony), and then returned to my home to spend a relaxing evening with my family so that I could be physically and mentally prepared for Sunday. Everything else was taken care of by the coordinator, who, according to the new policy, charged the couple an appropriate fee for her services payable two weeks prior to the wedding.

Furthermore, I began using a professional, credentialed marriage and family therapist to conduct all premarital counseling sessions for those wanting to be married in our church. I did this for two reasons. First, I recognized a competency skill that I did not possess. I am not a counselor. My wishes for happiness and blessing upon the marriages I conducted were sometimes short lived. If I was going to be a good minister to these young people in one of life's most significant times, I discovered that I needed to know how to refer them to a capable, skilled, spirit-filled minister of pastoral care. They had to pay for his services, but what they received in return was far greater than what I was capable of offering them.

The second reason I began doing this was that I recognized the distraction of trying to offer premarital counseling to so many couples. God had called me to pastor. Preaching was my primary responsibility, not counseling and coordinating weddings. If you are going to invest10 to 15 hours in a given week to your "wedding ministry," it is going to come out of the time you normally would give to your family, study, ministry of leading, personal growth, and your ministry of evangelism. Quite honestly, I grew tired of the distraction. Once I freed up my time in this one area by *enlisting and enabling* others to help me, I discovered a renewed passion for the things that truly were important.

This will prove true in every situation you face when you first develop your pastoral enlistment and empowerment list. The more you delegate by enlisting and enabling, the more passionate you will prove to be in the areas of your primary calling. You will be developing leaders in the process. You also will be building a team. Later, as your ministry grows, you will discover others who will be willing to be enlisted and enabled to perform the new ministries that God brings out of your church. Your congregation will appreciate your driven commitment to excellence. They will admire your willingness and resolution to equip the saints. They will feel a greater sense of ownership in the church. Should God call and lead you elsewhere, you will leave behind a team of ministers capable of continuing the ministry that God gave the church. That in itself becomes one of those immeasurable rewards that you have to experience firsthand to understand, but it is worth it when you do!

Church Administration

Administrating a church requires efficiency. It is a God-sized task regardless of the size of the church. The single-member pastoral team will find it impossible to effectively lead, let alone attend, every committee meeting that will come along in the life of the church. If at all possible, an *Administrative Ministry Team* should be established early in the administration in order to lead effectively.

Nowhere in the Bible will you find an effective committee outside of the Book of Acts. In chapter 6 there is a committee of individuals who were used to remove the dead bodies of the two liars in the church, but outside of this, there are no committees in the Bible who demonstrate effective leadership. The majority report of the Old Testament spies indicates that committees often are afraid of God's plan, and the committees in the New Testament are seen crucifying the son of God by orchestrating his arrest and mock trial. Why then do we have committee-driven churches throughout most of Christendom?

The answer is obvious. It is a way of getting a job done. Face it, pastor-leaders have moved from church to church so often that most church members had to look to lay leaders for any sense of consistency in performing the administrative duties of the church. Hence, we have committees.

Ministry Teams work better in the church. Using the *Ministry Gifts Inventory* found in *Kingdom Principles Growth Strategies,* a pastor can lead the members of a church to understand their spiritual gifts and can then begin to encourage the shift to ministry teams as an intentional response to the purpose statement developed by the congregation. When a team spirit has been nurtured by the pastor, this shift can become a reality with minimal difficulty. I think it is well worth the effort.

The Administrative Ministry Team becomes the *task force* that manages all of the church's administrative ministry. This includes all personnel, finance, and building maintenance issues. Members of the Administrative Ministry Team should have a passion for church administration backed up by a strong score in administration from the *Ministry Gifts Inventory.* Their selection should be based upon the qualification for church leaders found in Paul's writing to Timothy (with the exception of the gender specifics regarding the exclusion of women).

The Administrative Ministry Team works with the pastoral leadership of the church to perform the administrative tasks of the church. Seven members make up the Administrative Ministy Team. Half of the team rotates off every two years. A chairman is selected, and two members are charged with the responsibility of overseeing each of the three areas covered by the Administrative Ministry Team's assignment areas of personnel, finance, and building maintenance.

The advantage to this organizational shift is obvious. The pastor can give leadership to this group consistently without having to attend multiple meetings. You can select the seven most gifted individuals in the body for this team, providing strong, committed, and passionate leadership. In each meeting, therefore, all seven members are encouraged to provide insight into matters that are being discussed. These matters can be discussed intelligently and quickly because all administrative interests are represented at each meeting. In other words, if a Personnel decision is being made, the issues related to budget and finance can be discussed without needing to call a special meeting of a finance committee at a later time that month. If there is a property concern, discussions relative to its impact on finances or personnel can be addressed immediately.

The bottom line returns to the purpose statement and vision statements that have been developed by the church. If a committee structure exists in your church and it helps the church achieve her mission, you may not need to go to this model. If your church is hindered in doing what Christ wants done because of a dysfunctional committee structure, it is time to consider this biblical model for administrative leadership.

A Final Word

Everything you have read in this chapter is proven and time tested. Establishing priorities and developing a vision is a costly exercise, but not as costly as doing business in a way that frustrates and contradicts kingdom growth. You are going to pay a price to be a spiritual leader today. Why not invest yourself in the things that are going to bring the highest returns possible. Establish the disciplines that are going to sustain you, cultivate the relationships that will nurture you, and develop a vision that will motivate and protect you.

INTERACTIVE APPLICATION

What are the strongest disciplines in your life today?

____

____

What are you doing that will have a strengthening impact upon you if you should encounter a crisis in your life?

____

____

List by name the significant relationships you have cultivated in the past two years that are nurturing you today.

____

____

By way of contrast, what relationship or habit have you cultivated that is not going to prove valuable in the long run?

____

____

What is your personal vision statement?

____

____

How would you prove it?

____

____

CHAPTER 3

Recruiting New Team Members

I remember well the first addition I experienced to my ministerial team. We broke all the rules. There were only 16 members in this church when I became pastor. I was fresh out of seminary and had been on the field for four weeks. On the fourth Sunday morning a young couple attended our services for the first time. Immaculately dressed, this couple participated in the worship service by singing and either took notes or wrote notes during the sermon. During the invitation, the husband gave his wife that look that every preacher learns early to recognize; he nodded to his wife and the two of them stepped out of the pew and down the aisle to place their membership in our church.

I had spoken to the couple by phone when they called to find directions to our church. Transferred to our city with his job, I knew they had an interest in joining a mission church, and I knew the reputation of the great church from which they were coming. I stood to share this with our church as most pastors do following the invitation. Pride filled my heart because these were our first additions. They were young, good looking, and ready to serve with us. "If you're happy to see the Espinosas make this their church home," I said with great pastoral pride, "let them know by saying 'welcome!' " The thunderous echo made by the 16 members had not totally resounded off the wall when the oldest member of our mission church raised his hand and said those two words pastors hear with a certain shell-shocked reticence, "Brother-pastor."

I recognized Roy, our volunteer music leader. Roy loved the Lord, looked like Frank Sinatra, and played the trumpet. By virtue of these things he had been named song leader. Roy said, "I overheard the Espinosas singing during our worship service. He has a great voice, and I would like to make a motion that we call him as our minister of music." The motion received an enthusiastic second by the church treasurer, and everyone said "Aye" before I could manage to pick my jaw up off the floor. Thus began my experience as a team builder.

The situation could have been much worse. God blessed in spite of our ignorance and sent a real blessing in Steve and Norma. I knew such blessing would elude me the next time, so when it came time to say good-bye to Steve and Norma five years later, I did my homework and orchestrated a better strategy. I learned several lessons in the process of adding four additional pastors to my team over the next four years. Knowing when, what, and how to add pastoral team members is an art requiring spiritual insight and interpersonal skills. Some leaders and their congregations never succeed in developing these skills. Consequently they remain single-member pastoral team churches, forfeiting their future growth potential.

Win Arn in *The Church Growth Ratio Book* suggested that a staff member be added for every 100-150 people attending worship. This is a good number to use as an indicator for the need to add a new team member if for no other reason, it will provide a financial base for the new minister. A team builder knows when the church needs to add a new pastoral team member. Three of the timing indicators are: (1) untrained volunteers have faithfully carried the congregation about as far as possible in a given ministry responsibility, (2) the pastoral care needs are growing beyond the ability of the existing team, and(3) realizing the vision articulated in the purpose statement of the church will not be possible without the addition of a competency base not present among the existing team. The first two reasons are not salient points without the third reality.

Add the new team member to meet a prioritized need consistent with the strategic plans of the purpose statement of the congregation. When you begin to consider adding a new team member, go back to your purpose statement and the strategic plans that have grown out of it. Determine the best possible job description that will address the most important need facing your church. The most common mistake made by many churches is to commit scarce ministry resource dollars on the wrong ministry personnel.

In adding team members, it is imperative that you know the purpose of your church. Why are you in business? What are the specific goals you have for your church in the next 24 months? What ministry competence will best assist you to lead the church toward those goals? Before you invest in a long-term relationship with a new ministerial employee, recall the *Pastoral Enlistment and Enabling List* (Chapter 2). Does your church have competent volunteers who would be willing to minister in response to the growing needs if enlisted and enabled? If enlisted, would they possess the spiritual gifts, the technical expertise, and the congregational affirmation needed to help lead the church forward in its mission? If not, it is time to add a member to your pastoral team.

Who's on First?

Whom do you add first when building your team? This depends on the gift constellation and skill base that represents the team of volunteers who serve your church presently. Many churches have capable and gifted volunteers who can lead youth and children's ministries, worship, and even provide the support skills needed to manage the church office. At times, recognizing the personal investment being made and the long-term value being served, a church may provide a tangible expression to these volunteers through salary management. If you have no volunteers in any of these areas, you probably need to add an *administrative assistant* first.

The administrative assistant needs to be a person with strong personal relationship skills. This individual should have a strong clerical background, computer competencies, and organizational skills. The personal relationship skills are invaluable due to the first impressions this person will make about your church and your ministry on the telephone. While many people visited our church by dropping in on a Sunday morning after driving past our facilities or checking the yellow pages, we found most came after calling around and finding out what time the services were or getting other information from one of our office assistants. This ability to deal with people is of utmost importance.

This first assistant also will be crucial in enlisting others for various responsibilities in the growing congregation. She will assist you in responding to church emergencies and crisis situations. She will become sensitive to the spiritual battles that are very real in your church. You will find in the right assistant a valuable prayer warrior, a secretary, and a professional colleague. Do not allow yourself to become saddled with the wrong individual for this crucial ministry position. It would be better to do the work of an assistant yourself than to have the wrong person in this position.

What's on Second?

Give attention to your purpose statement before ever thinking about the next ministry team position to create. What is God calling your church to accomplish that will require the spiritual gift and professional training best found in an additional, paid, called, team member?

The most important ministry competence in a growing church may be organizational skills. This is especially true in a church that is experiencing growth and has a high growth potential. This organizer needs to have the skills of a coach. Being a trainer, encourager, and organizer, this first assistant will be a great asset to a pastor and the entire congregation. Meeting two primary needs, this minister will enable the church to "grow deeper through discipleship, and broader through ministry."[1] This may be a pastor with a religious education calling and the theological training needed for training others in teaching and leading.

Your church may need someone to work beside you in the area of worship leadership. A pastor with training in the creative arts of music and drama can minister effectively in growing the church "stronger through worship."[2] When the church grows stronger, more volunteers are usually willing to come forward in response to ministry needs that are being discovered in the body and the community.

Predictably, if this is the first full-time salaried position your church is considering, it may be wise to find a pastor with skills and training in more than one area. After finding an administrative assistant, our church began looking for a full-time minister to lead both the educational and music ministries of our church. We wanted someone who could show evidence of God's call in their life and someone who had completed formal training in the areas of music and religious education in college and seminary. We profiled the team position, first indicating every requirement necessary for calling; then we began looking for someone to fill the responsibility who matched the profile. God blessed our search process, and after several months of praying for the right individual, we found that person.

Following these two "high investment-high return" team members, a church will be in a position to consider other team members to lead other ministries. Becoming age-group conscious, or target sensitive, a church may go in any number of directions. The importance of the mission statement of the church and the spiritual giftedness of the congregation, superimposed over the community survey of the church mission field should dictate the next ministry role. Look to call someone with gifts and strengths to complement the existing weaknesses or deficiencies of your present team. The possibilities could include a minister of students and singles, a minister to families of preschoolers and children, a minister to senior adults, a minister to contemporary adults, a single adult minister, a minister of church recreation, a minister of discipleship, a minister of missions, a minister of church growth and evangelism, or a minister of pastoral care. Some churches have over three hundred professional team members leading their congregations. Space prevents me from mentioning every team member title possible.

The bottom line may not be "what to add next" but to answer the question, "How to add a team member."

What Are the Important Steps?

You will know when to add an additional team member by watching several indicators. First, as mentioned, *watch the numbers.* As your church increases in active, participating membership, it will become apparent that for growth to continue, the leadership team will have to be expanded. The strategic planning process of *Kingdom Principles Growth Strategies* will help determine a five-year planning model for the church. Within that planning model, there should be a plan to include additional pastoral team members as the active membership grows.

Watching these numbers, the pastor needs to help the other leaders within the congregation begin to pray about building the size of the team. Go to those God has put around you who are prayer warriors and together flesh out the vision for ministry. Share with them the progress the church is making toward certain goals and the ensuing need to bring the right team member on board to continue the growth process.

Begin sharing the progress with the deacons, Administrative Ministry Team, and volunteer team leaders. Let them know the direction you sense the Lord is leading the church. Receive their suggestions, but constantly project the image of the vision God has given you for the church. In open and honest dialogue, your vision may be refined, while the vision of others becomes more clearly focused and consistent with what God has impressed upon your heart.

The day will come when you need to present a plan to the entire congregation. Prayerfully, do your homework and humbly share the results of your prayers with the entire church family.

It is crucial to appeal to vision and to make the decision to add to the team a faith decision. In most cases when the team is being built in a church, the budget has to be stretched beyond its present ability in order to bring on another pastor. However, you will know that it is time to build the team when you look at the strategic plans before you, knowing that this added team member will be one of the crucial resources needed for your church to continue pursuing the growth plans.

Job descriptions: Do not attempt to add a team member until a job description is approved by the Administrative Ministry Team and presented to the church body. Some are calling this document a ministry covenant, others refer to it as a position content document. Whatever terminology you use, several key ingredients should be included.

The Title: Use a descriptive title for the position that best describes the primary responsibility that will be given to that team member. Such titles include, Minister of Music, Minister of Education, Minister of Youth, Minister of Missions and Evangelism, Minister of Pastoral Care and Counseling.

Introduction: I suggest using the following statement: "The Minister of Music will be a member of the Pastoral Team of this church and will be responsible to the Senior Pastor in fulfilling the following ministry tasks and expectations." Following this statement, the specific ministry tasks and expectations need explaining in no more than 10 statements, with a percentage of the time generally expected assigned to each task indicated.

Upon presentation of the Ministry Team Position and the Job Description, the *professional profile* developed for this position should also be presented. Many churches do not use a profile in filling ministry positions. This is a mistake. A profile sets a professional standard for excellence in the team building process. A profile helps prevent the promotion of incompetence and encourages hiring that balances gift vacancies and skill deficiencies of the existing team. Our churches need this discipline.

The profile will include the minimal expectations regarding Christian maturity, church experience, spiritual giftedness, educational background, and theological training necessary for the team position. The profile needs to have a range of spiritual gifts that would be evident in a person's life suited for this team position. Compare all résumés to the profile initially before ever considering a candidate. Prayerfully consider only the résumés of those meeting the profile for the team vacancy.

The Pastor-Search Team: Set aside a team of five to seven laypersons, and recognize them as the team that will search for the person God wants to use as the next pastoral team member. Include active members of the congregation, especially, but not exclusively, those with a passion for the specific ministry area needed. You have no quotas in putting this group together. You need the best, most trusted church leaders you have assuming this responsibility. They need to be the people in whom you confide. They may already be your prayer partners. They may be involved in leadership positions in the church already. They may include one of the spouses of another pastoral team member. You must select the best team if you want to find the best new team member.

When it comes to staffing ministry teams in the church there are two cardinal rules that I hope you already know and have committed as core values. First, do not put anyone in leadership who operates out of a hidden agenda. Second, never advance anyone to a crucial, high level position that can impact the future of your ministry in an attempt to appease or quieten them. These rules are vital in working with the group of people who will help you build your pastoral leadership team.

Bring the names of these individuals before your other pastoral team members (if you have others), and bring them before your deacons for prayer and affirmation. Finally, bring them before the congregation when you present the position, the job description and the profile so that the church will understand from day one something of the process in finding this new minister. Following their approval (if needed based on your by-laws), call the congregation to come forward and gather around members of this search team for prayer and encouragement. Keep the congregation committed to praying for this team until their task is complete.

A Biblical View of Adding to the Team

In adding a pastor to the team, emphasize Ephesians 4:11-16 as the rationale behind the process. You are building the pastoral team in order to build the body of Christ. Using the strategic planning process of *Kingdom Principles Growth Strategies,* prayerfully search for the mind of God. Adding to the team is an intentional response to the leading of the Holy Spirit in the process of fulfilling the Great Commission. It does not mean that the church can relax and let another do the work of evangelism and disciple making. It means that the efforts to become proficient in the Great Commission are taking a big step forward. The addition of the next team member will serve to equip the body for continued and deepening involvement, not less.

Financial Provision

The church body must be willing to assume a great responsibility in adding to the team. Providing for the new team member is a responsibility of the church. Address the salary issues, plus the responsibilities of providing appropriate benefits such as health insurance, automobile allowances, continuing education and professional development, retirement contributions, and convention-related expenses. Salary administration is the one tangible opportunity that a church has to express appreciation to a minister on an annual basis.

The most gracious way in which salary administration can be handled is to use an inclusive single line item in the church budget for all salaries. There are many reasons for this. First is a very practical reason related to the incentives of motivation and discipline. If a minister works hard and leads well, the work should be recognized by an appropriate raise. This would include a cost of living adjustment and a merit increase. Ministers do not work on commission. Overtime pay is never an option. (Defined by labor laws as anything over 40 hours a week). Offer raises that fall in a range that is appropriate with the salary range for the ministry position. Following an annual evaluation with the senior pastor, a recommendation should be given to the Administrative Ministry Team for the adjustment of a merit increase. (In the case of the senior pastor, the chairman of the Administrative Ministry Team and the chairman of the deacons perform the evaluation.) The cost of living adjustment should not be tied to the merit increase but is in addition to it.

There will be times when a minister needs to be disciplined through salary administration. There has not been an immorality, nor has there been sufficient need to terminate the minister. Instead, leading with grace and redemption, there should be a meeting with the appropriate individuals following the annual evaluation, (usually the senior pastor and the personnel leaders of the Administrative Ministry Team), and the minister should be told that his ministry performance has been sub-standard resulting in a zero merit increase, and, in some cases, no cost of living increase. In cases like this, it is not necessary to parade such action before the entire congregation. This causes speculation and rumor, in addition to hard feelings by those who may not be aware of the minister's evaluation. It is not advisable to give an "across the board" increase because it fails to recognize those who have served more faithfully than others while unfairly rewarding and encouraging continued slackness in ministry by those who are less faithful.

Some argue that by moving to a single line item in the budget for salary administration, members no longer have a voice in determining the raises for their ministers. During annual budget discussions youth ministry budgets have been increased, choir materials increased, debt reduction payments increased, and benevolent provisions increased, but never have I heard anyone from the floor seek to raise a minister's salary. My ear was bent by sincere parishioners often who told me they thought my salary was too low, but strangely they were overcome by speech impairments during budget discussions. I see the argument as hypothetical at best, in reality it is an unreal probability.

Others will accuse the leaders of trying to hide something and even claim that because their salaries are a matter of public record, so the minister's salary should be too. This short-sighted argument fails in its myopic comparison. In no other environment except ministry, do the families of professionals have to endure the monthly stress of having their household incomes published for every church member (and visitor) to read in a church business meeting. This is a monthly evaluation that no one else's entire family has to experience in a public forum. Those who insist on knowing the salary breakdown of the minister are only seeking yet another entrée into an arena of his life that is quite honestly none of their business. Churches have elected leaders entrusted by the congregation to handle these matters. These leaders are the ones who provide the necessary accountability giving the ministry its financial integrity when it comes to salary administration. It needs to go no further.

In all these matters, the passion I express comes from a conviction founded in the word of God.

> *Let the elders that rule well be counted worthy of double honour, especially they who labour in the word and doctrine.*

> *For the scripture saith, Thou shalt not muzzle the ox that treadeth out the corn. And, The labourer is worthy of his reward.* (I Tim. 5:17-18).

> *Remember them which have the rule over you, who have spoken unto you the word of God: whose faith follow, considering the end of their conversation* (Heb 13:7).

The workman is worth his wages according to God's word. The elder (pastor) is worth double honor, especially those to teach the word. Antagonists have a spiritual problem and have become pawns in a satanic strategy to oppress the church and distract the minister. They have no respect for biblical authority and have neglected the admonition to provide in a way that reflects honor and appreciation, let alone, financial responsibility.

When financially able, a church should seek to provide other resources that will help the pastor be effective such as computer hardware and software, cellular phones, beepers, or other communication tools that may be needed. It is a new day, and getting newer every day. The resources that will be usable in ministry five years from this writing may make the tools listed above obsolete. If businesses provide these tools for their workers to enable them to close a sale or more effectively respond to a customer or client need, so much more should the church.

Making the Search Meaningful

The Pastor-Search Team needs to spend an exorbitant amount of time in prayer. Before they ever engage in conversations with an individual, it is imperative that they have the mind of God regarding their responsibilities. They have a worthy task and must be completely reliant on the Holy Spirit of God if they are going to serve their church at this defining moment.

Request résumés from seminaries, other churches, members within the body, and denominational agencies. Once they are received, a member of the team needs to compare them with the profile eliminating those who do not meet the qualifications. After an appropriate time of gathering résumés, the entire team should begin to meet and no additional résumés should be reviewed.

Continue to saturate the process in prayer. Give each member of the Pastor-Search Team a copy of every résumé that matches the requirements of the profile. Engage in a brief discussion as team members respond spontaneously to observances they make about each résumé. Discuss a calendar for subsequent team meetings, and reinforce all expectations of Pastor-Search Team members during this initial meeting. The assignment for the next meeting (which should take place in one week) is to go through the stack of résumés prayerfully and come to the next meeting with a personal "top five" list based upon the experience base and training of the potential candidates represented by the résumé.

At the second meeting, this list needs to be shared secretly with the Pastor-Search Team secretary, (identified previously upon enlistment). The secretary compiles the results of this top five list and gives it to the team leader. If a trend emerges, say, three résumés are consistently in all top five responses, the group needs to proceed to talk specifically about these three. Discussion needs to center around what made these common "top five's" outstanding. Why were they chosen? What do we know about the training, experience, even former churches that would help us understand God's leading us toward them. If there are any "red flags" or hesitations, sufficiently deal with them in this meeting, or remove the résumé from further consideration.

The search will become more meaningful as the team continues in this process narrowing the potential candidates to a preferential list, in numerical order of the top three candidates. Depending upon the nature of the ministry position this candidate presently holds, the search team may want to visit the church on a Sunday to see this minister in a leadership role. Observe everything about the church. Everything that happens, or does not happen is in some way a reflection of the contribution this potential pastoral team member will have on your church. Following your initial visit, the search team needs to convene quickly to share impressions and continue praying about engaging this candidate. If everyone feels strongly about making a personal contact, proceed. If not, make plans to visit the church of the next potential candidate on the preferential list.

Eventually, the Pastor-Search Team Leader (identified previously upon enlistment) needs to make the initial contact, preferably by phone. With sincerity and graciousness, let the candidate know of your intentions and your impressions from having worshiped and observed his role in leadership. Share information about your church and your vision for the future of the church. Be prepared to respond to questions, and ask for permission to send some printed information about your church and your community to the candidate. This printed information should include the job description, salary and benefit schedule, a brief history of the church, a copy of the constitution and bylaws, the purpose statement of the church and the vision statements accompanied by a church calendar, a recent newsletter, a copy of a Sunday worship guide, and anything else to give the candidate a positive first impression about the church. Set up a time to call the candidate back in about a week, giving him time to receive the printed information you are going to send and to begin praying about things themselves.

In the next search team meeting, share the results of the first phone conversation. Indicate the candidate's openness to a ministry transition at this time. Continue to pray for the process, but make no further assignments unless the candidate has given you permission to investigate further. If you are scheduled to call the candidate back prior to the search team's next scheduled meeting, make the call short, informative, and encouraging. The candidate may not sense this is God's will at this time. If not, thank him and move on to the next potential candidate. If the individual is interested in pursuing the possibility that God is in this, let the courtship begin.

Courting a Potential Team Member

Another big mistake in recruiting new team members is getting in a hurry to add fresh blood to the team without taking time to court and get to know the candidate. If there is interest in pursuing an individual as a professional minister, a member of our team, a person who will impact our lives spiritually for a potentially long time, it makes sense to get to know them as intimately as possible. I recommend you court them for six months if at all possible.

How do you do that, especially when you wanted them on the field yesterday? You have to keep a Kingdom perspective. If God is in control, and if He already knows what is best for your church, don't you think He will guide you in the process and work out all the details? Take your time and avoid making the mistakes that are caused by rushing into things. Plan several more visits to the candidate's ministry setting by several groups.

First, let the search team go two more times on random Sundays to see the candidate and the church in more than one sitting. Their impressions may be different, or they may continue to be confirmed.

At some point, plan a visit with the candidate yourself. If you have other pastoral team members, take one of them along with you first. Plan a visit in a neutral setting somewhere near the candidate's field of service. This is just a get-acquainted visit. Ask questions about previous ministry settings, former pastors, seminary experiences, and so forth. Listen for the names of anyone the candidate may drop. Note them mentally so that you can follow up on them as references. Let your team member share in the discussions by talking about the vision for your church. You are not pressing for commitments in this meeting, but you are becoming acquainted. Provide the candidate with a copy of the *Ministry Gifts Inventory* from *Kingdom Principles Growth Strategies.* Ask the candidate to complete the *Ministry Gifts Inventory* and return it to you in the next couple of days. Provided you have already led your pastoral team to complete the *Ministry Gifts Inventory,* you will be able to see how this individual's spiritual gifts complement those on the existing team. Go back to the profile. Does this disqualify the candidate? If so, be honest. If not, proceed. When you leave from this visit ask, "Will I enjoy working with this person for the next 10 years or not?" If God impresses you that this is not the right individual, call your search team leader immediately and share that information. Remember, you have people on this team in whom you can confide.

Allow the candidate to visit you in your community. This is another informal, get-acquainted visit. If he is married, invite him to bring his spouse. If the visit will require motel, meals, and transportation expenses, provide those. While the candidate is in town, bring all of your team members and their spouses together for fellowship. You need to see this individual in a number of settings.

It is not improper to ask the candidate if he is leading a conference, revival, or workshop in the near future. If so, ask for permission to attend. This will provide you the opportunity of observing him in a ministry setting so that you can evaluate his abilities. If this is not possible, you may want to invite them to attend a professional workshop (at your expense) to give yourself another opportunity of seeing him in a professional environment. Throughout this process, you should have been receiving information from references. Barring no re-direction from the Holy Spirit, you are ready to proceed into more formal negotiations.

Invite the candidate to lead in an appropriate event in your church. You may have a study planned in which this person could speak, sing, or teach. You may want him to join you for a training event at your church. Listen for the feedback you receive from members of your church, especially those in leadership positions and your other pastoral team members. Set aside time during this event for formal interviews. Providing hospitality for the individual and his family is important. Err on the side of grace. Do more than is necessary. Meet every need humanly possible.

If all goes well, share with the church your intention of bringing this person to serve with you as a member of the pastoral team. Set a date to invite the individual back, this time, in view of a call. During an appropriate time in the worship service, plan for the candidate to share his personal salvation testimony and call into the ministry. Let him participate in some aspect of leadership during worship. In a spirit of worship, and as an act of commitment, let the team leader of the Pastor-Search Team share with the members of the church that it is their unanimous decision to bring this minister to the church for a vote to call him. Ask the church to stand if they are in favor of calling this candidate to the vacant team position. As they do, introduce the candidate as "Pastor"[3] by name, the new Minister of Music, or Education.

Steps to Transitioning

Be prepared to provide the moving expenses necessary to relocate your new team member. Allow the time necessary for the resignation from the present field of service. Know that this is a difficult time of saying good-bye to some precious friends. Be gracious in allowing for the sale of a home, the completion of a school semester if children are involved, and the establishing of "normal" household routines once the new team member physically relocates.

A thoughtful procedure is to *provide a Transitioning Team* to help welcome the new team member to the community. This team may provide assistance in locating good schools, a home, finding physicians and dentists, assisting with other transitional issues such as automobile tags and drivers license information, and voter registration. In a unique way, the transitional team can plan a series of fellowship events that will enable the new minister and family to become better acquainted with the church family in a steady and accelerated manner.

Allow time for the new team member to get his feet firmly planted with home and family issues. Being gracious at this point of beginning will prove to be a valued investment in the near future. If the new team member and his family believe you have their best interests at heart, they we serve beside you faithfully from day one. Take this time to be especially sensitive to the spouse of your new team member. Often the stress of such transitioning is compounded upon her shoulders.

Finally, provide a detailed orientation for your new team member. This should include reading church records, asking questions, visiting hospitals with you, and making evangelistic visits with you as soon as possible. Introduce the new team ember to the resources for ministry that you have found valuable, and include him in some of your fellowship groups with other ministers. Plan to be a full-time assistant for the first week, and be prepared to pull back slowly in the weeks to come.

If you are about to begin the process, keep soberly before you the reality that everything you do in the process of adding a new team member will affect everything you will do in the ministry of your present church for years to come. Putting the decision off delays potential blessing. Bringing on the wrong team member weakens the team, but when you honor God and the process works, your ability to build a team and impact the Kingdom multiplies.

---

[1]Rick Warren, *The Purpose Driven Church* (Grand Rapids: Zondervan, Publishing House, 1995), 49.
[2]Ibid.
[3]The rationale for using the term "Pastor" is discussed in Chapter 4.

CHAPTER 4

The Limited Team Partnership

Words carry the potential to color our perception about nearly everything in life. Ask the advertising executive who is working on a new marketing strategy. Ask the politician who wants to be elected. Ask the preacher who sits before the glare of a computer screen trying to tweak a line in a sermon or a phrase in a newsletter article. Words set stages. Words create environments. When it comes to choosing the words you use daily, time and attention is given to the precise selection of a poetic prose or an alliterative jewel. Pastors have mastered word selection as an art form. Team builders have too. Because of this, you will never hear them refer to the pastors with whom they serve as "staff."

Adding "staff" is the process whereby a church finds people to do the work that no one else wants to do for free any longer. Staff work for others. Staff are paid sub-standard wages for unappreciated tasks. Staff often show little loyalty because none has been modeled before or concerning them. There is a tremendous blight in churches today because they are infected with "staff," and the people in pews and pulpits expect nothing more. Until the situation changes, the church should be quarantined.

The leader's vocabulary tells more about leadership style than it does the character and competency of those with whom he serves. As consideration is given to increasing the work force in the local church, the leader needs to determine if he is going to be relational in his approach to others and build a team, or if he is going to be task consumed and build a staff.

Every pastoral team has its beginning. Pastoral teams increase in size depending on a number of circumstances. *The Limited Team Partnership* describes the early stages of multiple pastoral leadership in the New Testament Church.

A church experiences a defining moment when it calls its first pastor.

When the church experiences growth and passes the indicators for additional leadership, it again finds itself at a defining moment. Most churches have limited resources at this point. The decision to add a team member is characteristically a step of faith for the congregation and the pastor-leader. It is crucial to *limit the scope of responsibility of the new team member to the immediate priority* identified in the church's purpose statement. In this respect, the word choice is "limited."

The word "team" carries with it the philosophical understanding of a living, dynamic, goal oriented body. Teams are found in athletics. The analogies using teams are countless. Teams have a coach. Sometimes the coach is a player-coach. Some teams require more than one coach to effectively accomplish their purpose. The relationship between the pastor and a new pastoral leader must be viewed as a team or disaster is in the making.

When the church calls its first team member, it is possible that the relationship will be difficult. Church members often experience reservation accepting new leadership. At times, this new member of the pastoral team experiences a short tenure because of the unwillingness of the congregation to accept new leadership and the growth demands that necessitated new leadership. There are times when the new leader even becomes a threat (real or imagined) to the team leader. In cases like this, there is virtually no way for the leadership of the church to be effective. When pastor-leaders view the relationship as a team and project the image as a team before the entire congregation, the potential for transition and acceptance is increased dramatically.

Team builders are intentional about building relationships of trust with other members of the pastoral team. Often pastor-leaders share the quip "If I have to look over a guy's shoulder all the time to make sure he is doing the work, I don't need him." While this is true for the most part, it doesn't happen simply because a leader has committed this statement to memory. It is the result of building a relationship of professional trust.

Trust will come as the result of several things. First, there must be the recognition of the leadership core identified by Dr. Michael Miller in *Kingdom Leadership*. Dr. Miller focuses on the call, competencies, and character of the minister. When a prospective team member is considered, it is essential that the pastor-leader and the church be 100 percent convinced of these three core characteristics.

The call to ministry. Recently while visiting one of our seminaries, a student approached our reception area and began asking questions about what it means to be called into ministry. At first, we thought he was joking. It became painfully clear that he was not. Here was a young man, preparing himself academically for a career choice in ministry, who apparently did not have a clue about a clear sense of God's call to ministry. The only thing that made this situation worse, was that it became evident that his experience was not an isolated one. The reality is that our seminaries and colleges have granted scholarships (with faithfully invested mission dollars) to young men and women who have never been called into the ministry. Unfortunately, these career-pathed men and women emerge undetected as credentialed leaders, and our churches unsuspectingly employ them, issuing a congregational call to one who has yet to be called by God.

The team builder must be intensive in his investigation when it comes to discerning God's call of an individual. This call must have a testimony that is backed by a scriptural model of God's call. This does not mean that men and women will begin seeing burning bushes or blinding lights on the way to their Damascus-like life journeys. It does mean that men and women will be able to verbalize God's undeniable impression upon their hearts, an impression that has resulted in a surrendered life.

A second notable characteristic of the called individual is a gift that is uniquely theirs for ministry. A gift recognized by others. A gift that is enthusiastically embraced by one intent on changing the world. The team builder is capable of recognizing these gifted individuals and provides a creative environment that encourages the expression of the ministry gift and its development.

The Character of the Minister

Team builders communicate high expectations of the team members they gather around them. There is probably no greater expectation than in the area of a team member's character. Character affects the work ethic. It assures builders leave nothing to chance when building their teams. They investigate character references thoroughly, knowing that the consequences of past indiscretions by a new team member can come back with devastating results. They watch perspective team members and investigate them by asking detailed questions of those who know them.

The competencies for ministry. A fundamental mistake made far too often in the team-building process is the failure to call competency to fill our weaknesses. Pastors and church leaders need someone to serve with them. They think that finding someone with the same gifts, ideas, educational background, and experience level, will fit in well with the "present mix," making for a smooth transition and a functional team. Overlooked in this strategy is the fact that one person cannot do everything, and if cloned, what you end up with is a team of people who cannot do everything.

God's Word talks about the many different gifts found in the body. When all the gifts are used, ministry takes place in a beautiful way. In building a team, it is vital to look at the gifts and competency strengths of prospective team members and only hire those who complement our weaknesses. In doing this, we fill in the gaps of the pastoral team as a whole and position ourselves to more effectively minister and serve the congregation and the community.

To do this, the pastor needs to complete a spiritual gifts inventory. (A good resource is *Ministry Gifts Inventory* in *Kingdom Principles Growth Strategies).* In building the team, it then becomes helpful for him to consider prospective team members who have gifts that are different from those recognized as the pastor's strengths. Similarly, some team builders are using personality inventories, leadership style inventories, and a multitude of other instruments to evaluate the potential strengths and weaknesses that a person may bring to the mix of the team. As a minimum consideration, the *Ministry Gifts Inventory* needs to be used.

Keep in mind that you will broaden the scope of your constituency by building the team with individuals who represent various social profiles. Consider age as a significant factor. While not exclusively true, the effectiveness of a minister is stronger among those who range in ages 10 years his senior to 5 years his junior. In other words, if you are 40 years old, you will be most effective in ministering to those from ages 35 to 50 years old. Building your team with gifted and competent individuals who represent decadel age differences can significantly boost your total ministry capacity as a pastoral team. One of the most effective teams I have witnessed is a four-member, limited team partnership spanning five decades. This is a church that runs around two hundred in Sunday School. Their ministry focus is broad and they are making a tremendous impact upon their community.

The Confidently Called

Before we can discuss matters of trust and personal relationships, there is at least one further consideration to mention in building the limited team partnership. It is the glue in the relationships and enables real trust to be cultivated among the team. I call it "confident calling." Without having to ask, it has been apparent to me that the team members who have been the most effective in their ministry have a holy confidence regarding their calling and ministry gifts. Ministers of music had no desire to become preachers. Ministers of education had no ambition to knock the senior pastor out of his role. Preachers had no desire to be youth ministers. Instead, everyone understood their calling and were confident in who they were and who God wanted them to be.

It may be important early in the building process to determine the aspirations that a potential team member brings to the table. A favorite question for me to ask is "What do you see yourself doing in five years?" Not only can you envision the possible mentoring benefit that you could offer during the coming five years, you also would be able to understand something of the confidence this individual has in what God is doing in his life.

Building a Relationship of Trust

A pastor once wrote me about a potential team member and said, "I can trust him with my wife and my wallet." That is trust! The idea is a simple one: if you want to be able to trust others, you have to invest the necessary time to get to know them. Team members have to know that you have their best interest at heart. Once they know this, they will be willing to trust you more and more each day.

As this book began to work its way across my computer screen, countless horror stories have emerged about pastor-leaders who have "lost control" when it comes to leading their "staff." The berating and embarrassment go hand in hand with the attrition rate.

Having settled the issue of the "confident calling" it seemed rather natural to move beyond the possible notion that one of my team members wanted my job. Repeatedly, members of my team pointed to the desk in my study and reminded me that was one place they never wanted to sit. Furthermore, they had absolute respect and trust in the person behind that desk. None of this happened by chance or by accident, but without it, we would never have become a team.

Building a relationship of trust. Which word in that sentence is most pregnant? For me, it is the word "relationship." Once we add to the team, we are in relationship. The relationship may be healthy or it may become sick, but as long as we are together, we are related. The team encounters distrust throughout the week both in and out of the church. When the team comes together, it is time to refresh and renew the relationship so that we can model the power of personal relationships before our people.

John Maxwell once shared a strategy whereby he intentionally invited members of his pastoral team to spend time with him for the purpose of fellowship. No agendas regarding church business, no evaluations, no confrontations. Just pure relationship building. Is it any wonder he is so effective in his ministry as a developer of leaders?

Team builders are doing some rather unorthodox things today to build team spirit and trust among their colaborers. Using a multitude of recreational opportunities, pastoral teams are becoming intentional about scheduling some time to "play together" as a team. My last team tried to schedule time for the pastors and spouses to get together about quarterly. Whenever a member of the pastoral team or our support team had a birthday,we celebrated as a group by taking that person to lunch.

Establishing a Shared Ministry Philosophy

Two characteristics will be evident among successful pastoral teams of the future: First, they will share a philosophy of ministry that embraces the five functions of the New Testament Church. Dr. Gene Mims discusses these five functions in *Kingdom Principles for Church Growth* (Nashville: Convention, Press, 1994). They are *evangelism, discipleship, ministry, fellowship,* and *worship.* The second characteristic is an unapologetic commitment to excellence as these five functions are accomplished.

A shared ministry philosophy is a mutually held, fundamental agreement about the basics of how and why ministry is done in the local church. It encompasses the purpose or mission statement of the church and its supportive vision statements and goals. A ministry philosophy is the fleshed-out environment in which individual members of a pastoral team (and a church) interpret the incarnational reality of Christ's calling and the Spirit's equipping them for ministry in a given situation.

A cohesive approach to sharing the gospel of Jesus Christ comes from a shared philosophy of evangelism. Nurture takes place because the fellowship needs are addressed through ministries that seem to balance one another. Worship does not have to be manipulated to address needs, it feeds the spirit of the congregation, preparing it for need-meeting ministry. These things do not happen by accident. They are the miraculous results growing out of commitment to the principles belonging to the Kingdom of God.

A shared ministry philosophy is born in the heart of God-called pastors. It is a commitment to do certain things a certain way. It is difficult to explain outside of the dynamic call of God. He is the ultimate team builder. We do not build the teams anymore than we build the kingdom. It is His divine work. Knowing this, however, encourages our participation in what He is doing. We find ourselves desirous of doing only the best for His eternal kingdom and His glory.

If pastors recognize this, then it should enable them to see their team members in a different light. God called them and put them together. It is a sacred trust. It is almost as significant a relationship as marriage.

Pastoring Your Team Members

A senior minister should never expect a copastor, a member of the pastoral team, to carry out the caregiving functions of ministry, nor model the expected leadership patterns necessary to inspire and influence others unless that team member is being pastored in like manner. It will not happen. This underscores the reality that often is overlooked in building a pastoral team—that when additional team members are added, the senior pastor's workload is increased, not decreased. What many call staff supervision, is in reality the second time demand of the team leader. The first new time demand is pastoring the team.

Touch Base with the Team

Once a week, if not more often, it is essential for the team leader to gather the members of the team together and find out how they are doing. Once in a staff meeting, the letters HIG/AYA appeared on our agenda. We charted our way through the other familiar abbreviations, FTG's (First-time Guests), OOT's (Guests from Out of Town). It was an uncharacteristically short staff meeting and when we came to the letters HIG/AYA I said that these letters stood for "How's it going, are you alright?"

One of the pastors looked up, revealed a smile, and said, "Fine, thanks for asking." Then a remarkable thing happened. We began talking about personal things: how Sunday really had been evaluated by our families and how some people were really difficult to get along with. We laughed, we shared, we took a few notes for our respective prayer lists, then we dismissed. The impact was clear. The pastors with whom I worked understood that they were important and that I truly cared for them.

Showing concern for the members of your team is like showing concern for the members of your family. The one minimal, tangible expression of our concern could be the one thing that enables a team member to get through a particularly difficult time.

In some churches, budget planning/adoption time is a pleasant, noneventful experience, yet it can be stressful. This time in a church year usually is filled with long committee meetings, long staff meetings, annual reviews and personnel evaluations. Once the budget is mailed to every member, the atmosphere can change to one of intense speculation, suspicion, harsh glares, anonymous letters, irate phone calls, and called deacons meetings. It is incredibly difficult on the minster's marriage. A spouse in ministry has to be subject to the annual approval or disapproval of a mate, the constant "wait and see" reality of how much their spouse is appreciated, and the annual motion to amend the budget offered by someone who "loves the minister" but feels this raise is out of line when compared to corporate America. The one tangible expression of appreciation that could be given by a church to a minister often is the single most cause of stress, pain, and drudgery that anyone called to a church will ever experience.

Knowing this, a senior pastor has the golden opportunity of ministering to the team by simply asking the questions relating to their personal welfare. It does not have to be much, but by listening to the hurts and frustrations, understanding the financial hardships, and reassuring the team member, a senior pastor can exercise the greatest mentoring and the most effective encouragement at the most vulnerable time in the life of the team.

CHAPTER 5

The Multimember Team

The excitement of seeing God's faithfulness demonstrated in growth and vitality of the local congregation is its own reward. God builds in spite of us, but God also is building through us. Not a point of pride, but a humbling reality rises from deep within the heart of the senior leader knowing that God is faithful.

Team-building pastors love to see God grow His church. There are multi-dimensional aspects of church health that result from applying Kingdom Principles.[1] Churches grow larger, deeper, stronger, broader, and warmer as they focus on evangelism, discipleship, worship, ministry, and fellowship.[2] We are no longer talking only about growing bigger churches, even though that is part of a worthy goal. We are talking about growing healthy churches. Gene Mims and Rick Warren are but two of the strong voices today reminding the leaders of the church that growth needs to be balanced and healthy.

One of the healthy indicators of a balanced, growing congregation is a pastoral team that is structured to meet the needs of growth by equipping the members of the congregation to do the work of the ministry. Pastoral care concerns, pastoral leadership, and pastoral administration go through several stages of change and adaptation in most growing churches. The way things were done in a church averaging two hundred in worship are different than the way things are done in that same church when it breaks the five hundred barrier. Not only are there differences in how the church ministers, there are differences in who does the ministry.

When the pastoral team experiences the addition of the fourth team member, there are some major shifts in how things are going to be done. The pastor becomes a player coach instead of a one-man team. His ministry has the opportunity to be increased by multiplication instead of by addition. To do this, the pastor has to pull the team in close assuming the role of coach, while pushing away some of the responsibilities that were once his when he was a one-man team. In some places, this shift in ministry leadership style is welcomed and encouraged. In some places it is not. Before a team builder finds himself working through the criticisms in a church where this leadership style is not preferred, it is crucial to establish a purpose statement and a corresponding set of vision statements that will enable and empower the principle of multiplied ministry influence.

Unfortunately, most pastoral job descriptions do not include anything remotely empowering or enabling. They may say "lead the staff" but in the mind of the average reader in our church, this translates, lead by example and do the work of the church with increased productivity since you have lots of help. The reason for this mental attitude is two-fold. First, congregations have little vision for the principle of multiplication. Second, for years pastors have not challenged the congregation's lack of vision by offering anything better. Singlehandedly, we attempt to do the work of the ministry and look with a jaundiced eye at our professional team members wondering why they are not as passionate, driven, and productive as we think we are.

Team builders envision a different relationship. The team builder says "I led the church to call this individual, now I should develop him so that the church will be blessed and more effectively ministered to, eventually wanting to call another team member, and another, and another." Leading is not saying "go and do" it is saying "come and let me show you how."

Mentoring Your Team

In the most effective congregations today, team-building pastors literally are discipling their team members. I read once years ago about an insurance company that required sales agents to mentor new agents for a period of one year. During this year, experienced agents take new members of the sales team with them on prospect calls, follow-up sales appointments, customer service calls, and a host of other related field events. Time after time it was shown that the sales for the senior agent increased over his previous earnings during the time when he was involved in the one-year mentoring program.

The reason is obvious. When mentoring or showing how to close a sale, the senior agent became more driven to close. When mentoring the importance of making customer service calls and "after-the-sale" follow-up calls, the senior agent was far more intentional, paying attention to every detail so that the new agent would be able to learn the lesson with power and enthusiasm. During the mentoring process, customers were blown away by the outstanding service and individual concern that seemed to be given to their need.

When I read this, it dawned on me that I was missing a great opportunity and blessing by not mentoring my team members with the same passion and intensity that this particular insurance company did. By carrying new team members along with you for one year, you train them in your philosophy for pastoral care, evangelism, and administration. You not only coach them in everything you want them to do, you also become more effective in the process because you will be increasingly passionate and driven in your desire to show new team members how. It's so simple. You will cultivate your prospects and anticipate a "closing" and bring along a team member so they can see how to do it themselves.

I took a new team member with me once for several months before encouraging him to take others or go alone. After serving with this team member for over five years, he knew me so well that we practically thought alike. Years later, we still enjoyed making outreach calls together. At the same place, there were two team members with whom the relationship was not as intentional. Consequently, I never saw them develop the same passions and intensities. Our relationship seemed to be one characterized by my constant attempts to convince. Convince them to visit. Convince them to minister in the same way I did. Convince them to take certain stands. You will frustrate your team members by trying to lead this way. They will want to please you but will not really understand how until they have caught it firsthand from being with you.

Mentoring is a great buzz-word these days, but what does it really mean? In the past, "mentoring" was a word used almost like a diploma hanging prominently on our study walls displayed for the exclusive purpose of impressing others. We would work sentences into otherwise good conversations such as "I was mentored by so-and-so" or "when I was in college, so-and-so was my mentor."

A shift in the emphasis of mentoring came along in the late 1980s and early 90s. Instead of the pretentious "me-centered" conversations about mentoring, we began to develop a little integrity, and with no fanfare or discussion, we began mentoring others. Bobb Biehl's excellent book, *Mentoring:*

Confidence in Finding a Mentor and Becoming One, should be required reading for every potential team-building pastor.

The benefits for mentoring our team flow directly from the word of God.

> *And the things that thou hast heard of me among many witnesses, the same commit thou to faithful men, who shall be able to teach others also. (2Tim. 2:2)*

The word "commit" is a mentoring word. In Paul's mind, the idea may have been "to make a deposit," but I think it involves more. The *New American Standard Bible* suggests the word "entrust." The imperative verb form gives Timothy (and us) no choice if faithfulness is desired. The word in its original language is used to describe the act of setting something, like food, in front of another person.

The imagery is pregnant with meaning! We love to sit at a fellowship table and enjoy a good meal. This is why real mentoring often takes place in the classroom of the coffee shop instead of steady academic environments. Mentoring involves placing a balanced meal before a growing and hungry individual. The mentor's words wrapping his experiences are seasoned and cooked to order. Mentoring feeds because it nurtures and enriches. Mentoring builds and encourages. Mentoring addresses specific needs by drawing pictures from the well of life's experiences. Mentoring is grace motivated and because of this, it intersects the life of the individual at a moment of craving ,and it satisfies like a home-cooked meal.

We can draw further images from Paul's mentoring passage relative to our team members. They are to be "faithful and able" or "reliable and qualified." Michael Miller would say "individuals possessing character and competency" *(Kingdom Leadership).* Hopefully, you have surrounded yourself with team members who exemplify these qualities. Inherent in Paul's imperative directive is the responsibility on our part to find the right people before whom we will place a mentor's delicacy. Remember, team builders know how to find the right people. They see character traits and have a spiritual gift in discerning giftedness in others. Find them. *Then find the time to multiply your ministry by mentoring them.*

Great Expectations

In an interview once, a senior pastor and incredibly gifted team builder repeatedly told me "we have great expectations for the individual who will be called to this position." God called me to another place, but He has never let me forget those words.

Every potential team member needs to be told that great expectations await them if called to serve in the local church. Why not? After all, the people of God who make up the church deserve the best leaders possible. What, then, are the fair and reasonable expectations a senior pastor should have of his team members?

Loyalty. A team member must be loyal. This loyalty is first experienced as loyalty to Christ, but it is unquestionably demonstrated as loyalty to the senior leader. Team members are going to hear virtually every criticism offered by church members regarding the senior pastor. From the pattern selection of the senior pastor's tie, to the ridiculous accusations regarding his bully pulpit, team members will find themselves the apparent confidant of well-intentioned and some not-so-well-intentioned members of the church.

Loyalty to the team builder will not require telling him everything heard. It will require that team builders become known as ones who will not listen to petty complaints. It also will require that team builders become ones whose standard interruption in the midst of both the petty and legitimate complaint be "Excuse me, but what you are telling me is something you really need to take up with your pastor, personally. If he wants me to know about it or if he needs my opinion, he will ask me for it. Until then, I cannot continue to listen to what you are saying. Go to him and tell him what you are telling me."

It is amazing how many things will never go any further. Obviously, there may be incidents when someone is coming to you with a critical issue and they really need your counsel and prayer support. Be discerning, but always be loyal. Never take sides. Never empower a grievance by lending a listening ear.

Hard Work. Team builders have every right to expect the members of their teams to share their work ethic. The work ethic needs to be clearly communicated in the interview process and confirmed in the reference-gathering process prior to extending a call.

One of the common criticisms expressed among senior leaders pertains to the relaxed work ethic of their staff. When asked for clarification, the answers include: lack of evangelistic passion, lack of pastoral care involvement, hard to motivate, last in the office, first to leave, and slow to volunteer.

The best way to motivate hard work usually is to model it. The annual review is also a helpful way in which to communicate the consequences of laziness. If members of the team are consistently ineffective due to their failure to understand what is expected of them, the team builder may need to evaluate the communication of goals and time management skills that are anticipated. An employee development training process could be outlined following a constructive evaluation of the team member's productivity.

Avoid becoming a disgruntled leader. This normally leads to the termination of a potentially effective team member. You have already invested the resources necessary to bring the member onto your team. If you discover some productivity issues, work to resolve them. You will end up with a stronger team member, you will practice a biblical form of redemption, and you will make a friend for life who will, in turn, multiply your ministry, not detract from it.

Integrity. There is no room for moral lapse on any level of leadership in the church. Unfortunately, it happens every day. Team members need to know that the expectation is for moral purity among every level of leadership in the church. Integrity and holiness are not synonymous, but where you find holiness, you will find people of integrity. Team builders do not assume that team members automatically strive for holiness. Therefore, they teach it and model it.

The consequences for moral failure in the church need to be clearly spelled out from the beginning. This way, no one can say they didn't know. While forgiveness and restitution is possible in some cases of moral failure, the church and the team member must understand that continued service and ministry may not be possible. Assessing the damage done is only a part of evaluating the total picture. Much greater damage to the reputation of the church and its Christian witness may be done in the future when a biblical pattern of church discipline is not carried out completely. In these situations, a redemptive spirit from the team builder is crucial. Never try to hide or cover up an integrity issue. Deal with it honestly and openly, seek to be redemptive, and move forward.

Spiritual strongholds can permanently impact future generations in the life of a congregation when they are not confronted and confessed. These strongholds may be temporarily vacated, but their presence in the life of the congregation will negatively impact future generations of leaders. Team builders are concerned with the future team just as much if not more than they are the team they presently lead. Team builders are visionaries. They are planting a seed that will one day grow into a mighty shade tree, the branches under which they will never sit. No one will ever want to take refuge where the shadow of an oppressive cloud of lost integrity hangs.

And Finally Brethren . . .

Paul concluded his letter to the Thessalonians in the same way this section will close. He articulates several bullets of vital importance to the church with little comment. The members of any team would do well to hear the following "expectation bullets" and apply them personally:

- Keep your relationship with Christ your first priority
- Stretch yourself mentally
- Never stop growing spiritually
- Be friendly and courteous
- Be on time
- Be professional
- Be prepared
- Be a servant

The Value of Projecting a Unified Image

Strange as it may seem, working with the team members you recruited can become tenuous and stressful. The reason relates directly to the satanic orchestrations that God's Word calls spiritual battles. We may add to the difficulties our own baggage of emotional scars and fears, but the root of the difficulties is fertilized with the fodder of Satan's desire to wound the body of Christ at every opportunity.

When the pastoral team is united, you provide a ministry to the church that cannot be provided in any other way. *People are encouraged and are made to feel secure when they see their spiritual leaders working and walking together as a united team.* One of the strengths mentioned earlier in making the choice to refer to every team member with the term "pastor" is that it creates the mind-set among the congregation that the team is united, colloquial, interdependent, and committed to one another in Christ as equals.

One way to keep this ministry from touching the lives of people in your church will be to fall prey to the plans drawn up by the author of confusion himself. If Satan can enable us to feel anger, resentment, bitterness, jealousy, pride, envy, or in some cases lust or covetousness toward a member of the team, it becomes instantly noticed by those who look to us as spiritual role models each week.

When you know that God is blessing and using your team, you also become increasingly aware of the reality of spiritual battle. The manifestation of this rarely is as severe as seeing your youth pastor's head spin around. However, if you do not trust him and find yourself one step away from distributing his résumé, the effect is about the same. If you are harboring resentment against a team member who has recently killed a Goliath with only a sling while you contemplated the possibility of surrender, then the people in your pews probably see the daggers in your eyes, if not the spear in your hands.

Flesh. We have to die to flesh daily. A little bit of pride may not kill us, but it will destroy the ministry. You know that the flesh is not dead yet when interpersonal differences rise and create tenuous atmospheres in what should be a grace motivated environment. *The crisis facing pastoral teams in our churches today are not theological differences. They are interpersonal differences.* Preferences gone awry. The refusal to seek peace. The stoic, immovable, impenetrable heart. Professional jealousies.

God's Word is plain on these issues. Have you ever wondered why there is so much in the Word of God dealing with interpersonal relationships? Care to count the passages that deal with forgiveness and reconciliation? Maybe they appear on nearly every page because God knew how often we would need to be confronted by them. Better yet, notice how often Paul refers to the various members of his expansion teams, those in prison and those on the outside, as his fellow laborers. Regardless of circumstances, they are in relationship!

A Motivation for Relational Leadership

There is little doubt that the spiritual revival everyone is beginning to talk about is possible. As we approach the year 2000 and the new millennium, people are going to be raising new spiritual questions that will point them to the church. If our relationships are right when they look in on us, we will be able to point many of them to Christ.

Read these passages and try to hear Paul's voice dictating a letter with his fellow laborers close by his side. Imagine the affirmation. Listen to Jesus' words from the sermon on the mount as though you are hearing them for the first time. Let the words from James roll across your mind and into your heart as you superimpose them across the faces of the members of your pastoral team.

> *Now I exhort you, brethren, by the name of our Lord Jesus Christ, that you all agree, and there be no divisions among you, but you be made complete in the same mind and in the same judgment .(1Cor. 1:10)*
>
> *Greet Prisca and Aquila, my fellow-workers in Christ Jesus. (Rom. 16:3)*
>
> *Greet Andronicus and Junias, my kinsmen, and my fellow-prisoners, who are outstanding among the apostles, who also were in Christ before me. (Rom. 16:7)*
>
> *Greet Urbanus, our fellow-worker in Christ, and Stachys my beloved. (Rom. 16:9)*
>
> *Timothy my fellow-worker greets you; and so do Lucius and Jason and Sosipater, my kinsmen. (Rom. 16:21)*
>
> *For we are God's fellow-workers; you are God's field, God's building .(I Cor. 3:9)*
>
> *As for Titus, he is my partner and fellow-worker among you; as for our brethren, they are messengers of the churches, a glory to Christ. (2 Cor. 8:23)*
>
> *So then you are no longer strangers and aliens, but you are fellow-citizens with the saints, and are of God's household. (Eph. 2:19)*

As to all my affairs, Tychicus, our beloved brother and faithful servant and fellow-bondslave in the Lord, will bring you information. (Col. 4:7)

Epaphras, my fellow prisoner in Christ Jesus, greets you, as do Mark, Aristarchus, Demas, Luke, my fellow-workers. (Phil. 1:23-24)

If possible, so far as it depends on you, be at peace with all men. (Rom. 12:18)

So then let us pursue the things which make for peace and the building up of one another. (Rom. 14:19)

Blessed are the gentle, for they shall inherit the earth. Blessed are the peacemakers, for they shall be called sons of God. (Matt. 5:5, 9).

Finally, brethren, rejoice, be made complete, be comforted, be like-minded, live in peace; and the God of love and peace shall be with you. (2 Cor. 13:11)

Being diligent to preserve the unity of the Spirit in the bond of peace. (Eph. 4:3)

And beyond all these things put on love, which is the perfect bond of unity. And let the peace of Christ rule in your hearts, to which indeed you were called in one body; and be thankful. (Col. 3:14-15)

But we request of you, brethren, that you appreciate those who diligently labor among you, and have charge over you in the Lord and give you instruction, and that you esteem them very highly in love because of their work. Live in peace with one another. (I Thess. 5:12-13)

For where jealousy and selfish ambition exist, there is disorder and every evil thing. But the wisdom from above is first pure, then peaceable, gentle, reasonable, full of mercy and good fruits, unwavering, without hypocrisy. And the seed whose fruit is righteousness is sown in peace by those who make peace. (Jas. 3:16-18)

INTERACTIVE REFLECTION

When is the last time you purposely sought to encourage a member of your team by telling them about a positive observation you made in their ministry?

___

___

Would the members of your pastoral team look back in 20 years and say that you were a strong mentoring influence in their lives?

___

If you answer yes, list the reasons why:

___

___

If you say no what do you see as the hindrances to this happening?

___

___

___

What are you willing to do about it?

___

___

Have you shared your expectations with the members of your pastoral team?

____

What expectations would you add to the bullet list?

____

____

____

Are you living at peace with all of the members of your team?

____

If not, will you make a commitment right now to change the relationship?

____

____

____

____

[1]Gene Mims, *Kingdom Principles for Church Growth* (Nashville: Convention Press, 1994).
[2]Rick Warren, *The Purpose-Driven Church* (Grand Rapids: Zondervan Publishing House, 1995), 49.

CHAPTER 6

Supervision Is Ministry

There is more to being a pastor than preaching sermons. There may not be anything we enjoy doing more than preaching, but there is more to pastoring than preaching. If you are in a building program, you have to give enormous blocks of time to overseeing, envisioning, motivating, sometimes even hammering and painting, but it is a part of ministry. What you do will matter years from now when you are no longer on the scene to see those being ministered to in the building. In this sense, building is ministry.

In the same way, supervision is ministry. There is only so much one person is capable of accomplishing when doing the work of ministry alone. There is no limit to the amount a person can accomplish when supervising the work done by dedicated team members committed to the same vision. This is true in the armed services where one officer is given supervisory responsibility for an entire regiment or battalion of soldiers. It is true in athletics when one coach supervises the work of multiple coaches and in turn, vast numbers of athletes. It is nonetheless true in the local church when the team builder discovers that supervision is ministry.

Team-building pastors have a style of supervision that is blended with mentoring. Webster's Dictionary defines mentor as "a trusted counselor and guide." Team builders work early to earn the trust of team members. They continue to protect that trust-giving counsel over the course of the relationship. Bobb Biehl defines mentoring as "a lifelong relationship, in which a mentor helps a protégé reach her or his God-given potential."[1] While few team members view the potential of a lifelong relationship at first, when the relationships are right, it invariably results in this kind of commitment. Biehl goes on to say "Mentoring is a relationship with someone you like, enjoy, believe in, and want to see win in life."[2] What an incredible ideal for the kind of relationships that are possible among those who serve Christ together day in and day out in the local church.

Doran McCarty wrote: "Supervision is a serious ministry. In fact, it may be the most significant that ministers perform during their own ministry, as they mold the lives of future representatives of and ministers in the Kingdom of God. They are almost the human mothers and fathers of ministers. They are the ones who rock the spiritual cradle to shape the future world of ministry. Therefore, this ministry of supervision should be approached with seriousness, commitment, skills and prayer."[3]

The realization that supervision is ministry saved my life once while pastoring during a growth cycle in a local church and community. I supervised the work of the pastoral team which consisted of three other pastors. In addition to this, I also supervised the work of four seminary students conducting Praxis work in our community for the purpose of starting two new churches. This required the selection process of two new pastors to lead in the mission work and with that, the supervision of everything they did. A college student intern worked with me for the summer doing pastoral ministry and some preaching. I supervised his work. I taught preaching classes for one of our seminary extensions and supervised the work of eight preaching students for two semesters. As though this was not enough, I also served as the field supervisor for a Doctor of Ministry student who was in the midst of his studies.

Instead of being overwhelmed with 20 supervisory responsibilities, I became encouraged by seeing the combined impact of 20 supervisory relationships. This experience in supervising ministry professionals became invigorating. We worked in tandem toward a common goal. It is impossible to really estimate the combined results of our team's efforts. Together, the 20 of us accomplished much more than one person could accomplish in years. Team builders know the thrill of multiplying their ministry, and they know that the price of the thrill is good supervision.

The imprint or influence of my ministry was multiplied numerous times in that one year. It was without a doubt the most productive year of ministry in that community in the 10 years that I spent there. But make no mistake about it, supervision was required.

How do you supervise others? Where do you start? What if you enter a vacant pastorate where a ministry team has been in existence for some time?

How do you earn the right to supervise in a meaningful way? These valid questions require vital answers.

If you are on the front end of team building, it is easier to write in to the ministry covenants or job descriptions a phrase or two specifying that supervisory responsibilities belong to the senior pastor. (See the sample ministry covenants/job descriptions included on the accompanying disk.) If you inherit a pastoral team, be certain that the lines of accountability are clearly drawn prior to your acceptance of the call to pastor. They will not be drawn after your arrival without a struggle. If the church fails to provide for this supervisory ministry, know up front that the last thing they want (including the staff) is a team builder. Your acceptance of such a situation will result in a difficult transition and an impossible environment for the development of any significant leadership. It will not be impossible. God may have indeed called you to bring about a needed administrative change.

When you accept a call to a church that has a ministerial team in place, and the expectation is that you will supervise the team, you are at least positioned for a role of ministry supervision. What you do in the first few days with this new team will determine your future effectiveness as their supervisor. It does not happen in every church due to our ineffectiveness and lack of protocol in accomplishing the work of pastor-search committees, but occasionally a prospective pastor has the opportunity to formally and informally meet with existing team members. During these meetings, supervisory relationships and expectations should be clearly defined and understood.

A disturbing trend is taking place in the CEO model of pastoring regarding the transition of a new pastor to a church with an existing pastoral team. The trend is to expect written resignations from every member of the team on the new pastor's desk on the day or shortly after the day he arrives. I understand this rationale from a secular business viewpoint. I do not understand it from a biblical viewpoint of the call of God and the related call from the church. The only way you can validate this practice is to assume that the existing team was called by the previous pastor and is a part of his ministry. If this is the case, the previous pastor should have made arrangements to carry "his team" with him as he made his exit to a new church field.

The "call" is issued by the local church having recognized a ministerial candidate's giftedness to meet a need in that congregation according to their purpose and vision statements. It is a recognition of the provision made by

God to send the right person to the church at a given time. It is therefore up to God to call that person away to a new field of service upon completion of his ministry in that church. It is the height of pastoral presumption to enter a new ministry setting and determine that the existing pastoral team should leave, or worse, play games with their emotional and spiritual lives by keeping undated resignations on file to use at a future time when they are considered disposable. Such policy is unbiblical and such methodology is unhealthy. It produces paranoia and cultivates followers motivated by intimidation rather than ministerial integrity.

A far better practice is to move into a new field of ministry and take advantage of the professional insight available from those on the team who have been in the church. They know the people. They are familiar with the resources for ministry. Unless they display incompetence early, they need to be commended for their role in keeping things going during the time the church was without a pastor. They can provide an instant circle for support and fellowship as you find become acclimated into a new place of ministry.

Basics of Supervision

It is precisely here that we start with the basics of supervision. Your ability to supervise is directly related to your ability to build relationships with your team. Intimidation will provide you with a level of respect that is static, forced, less than genuine, and unfulfilling to all involved. Supervision that is built on a relationship characterized by trust, respect, and affirmation will prove far more beneficial in the long run. We are not CEOs, we are pastors. We have a biblical model to follow. When we follow this model, we become grace leaders and team builders. Here's how.

Within the first four weeks of your arrival to a new field of service, or within the the orientation process of a new team member, you need to schedule three appointments with each individual team member. The first is an informal interview. During this time, ask a series of important discussion questions such as:

- What do you think the top three priorities of our church should be right now and why?
- How would the people in our church answer that question?
- What can I do to help you accomplish your top three professional or personal goals in the coming six months?

- Where are you struggling in your work?
- What are you doing to nurture yourself spiritually, mentally, emotionally, and physically?
- How can I pray for you in the coming month?

Take no notes during this interview; it is informal. Listen with your eyes. Mirror the answers back in conversational form to your team member so that you will make sure you understood and so you will be better able to remember what was said. Following this interview, you may want to go back and make some notes for yourself, but start off by being relational, not formal.

A second valuable informal meeting will be a time for you to host members of your team in an informal setting in your home. Due to the variables you will encounter with moving (if you are new) this may be difficult to do in the first month. However, as soon as you can, try to offer this genuine show of hospitality to the members of your team and their spouses. The relaxed environment will provide opportunity for you to get to know one another better. Again, *one of the keys to building a healthy team is relationships.*

By the fourth week of your ministry on the new field, or during the official orientation of new team members, you need to have a formal meeting to discuss supervision. Do not use the pastoral-team meeting for this. You already have a detailed agenda that will require extended time and energy. Instead, choose a time when you can call the entire team together, or those being oriented, and schedule enough time to cover the scope of your supervisory responsibilities and expectations.

Supervision takes place weekly. In every pastoral team meeting you are supervising the work of those called to minister alongside of you. This is a time for direct guidance and instruction. It also is a time of colloquial planning and discussion of ministry opportunities. As the leader of the team, you need to give weekly direction and oversight to the work of the team.

Create an environment where team members will want to share reports of their ministry. One of the best ways to do this is to enthusiastically look at what you are doing in your ministry. Discuss the results of your visitation ministry. Share the non-confidential prayer requests from members in the congregation that have come to your attention. Compare notes on the answers to prayers and the challenges that are before you. Talk about victories won and scheduled events on your calendar. Let your team know what you are doing. Then ask for a member of the team to give a similar report. As everyone has an opportunity to share, supervision takes place in its basic form. They report to you, and you have the opportunity of encouraging, correcting, affirming, or challenging anything in the report. Other team members see what is happening and the level of accountability grows.

A second form of supervision is informal. It is supervision by peripheral participation. Get permission from the pastor who directs the Music Ministry and make an informal visit during a choir rehearsal. Tell the education pastor that you'd like to observe his next teacher's meeting and then informally drop in. In both of these arenas, you can say a word of appreciation to the groups involved, thank them for the support they give your team member, and then stick around for a few moments and watch the team member leading this group. Similarly, surprise the youth minister by volunteering to chaperone the next youth event planned at church. Do not get in the way by trying to lead an event, just be in the background and observe everything you can.

Formal supervision includes things like the annual review. Countless methods exist for performing such reviews. Some churches expect the pastor as supervisor of the pastoral team to conduct these reviews, others use committees for this purpose. Regardless of the method, the pastor as supervisor needs to have input into the annual process as it deals with salary administration or other tangible expressions of affirmation or correction.

Pastoral-team members need to be evaluated and supervised in the following three areas.

Job Descriptions and Performance Reviews
Personal and Professional Goal Accomplishments
Ministry of Personal Relationships

Job Descriptions and Performance Reviews

Annually, team members need to review a copy of their job descriptions. Discussing the job description with the supervisor, they need to determine if it adequately reflects the work they are expected to do. On a scale of one to five, (one being the lowest, five being the highest) team members and the supervisor need to rate the performance of each area listed on the job description. When the numbers are close or the same, this is cause to speak about the obvious strengths or weaknesses observed in each team member's performance and to become affirming or prescriptive in making plans for the future. When the numbers are further apart, it is a great opportunity to discuss either the potential hidden dangers to the team member's ability to support the team's vision, or the obvious weaknesses in the team member's competency base.

Team members should know that a peer review is available following an annual review with the supervisor in the event that they feel they have been given an unfair evaluation. Individual churches no doubt have a procedure for such events using personnel committees, deacons, and administrative ministry teams. It is unethical and extremely poor stewardship for a church to determine salary administrative issues without an annual review for individual team members. It also creates an impossible expectation for motivating members of the team to increase their skills and broaden their ministry goals.

Personal and Professional Goal Accomplishments

At the annual review, team members need to be asked to formalize personal and professional growth goals. This provides an opportunity for individual team members to plan for growth to take place in their personal lives. They can identify areas of weaknesses from the performance review and become intentional in trying to add new strengths. The church may provide your team members with a budget for seminars, conferences, or other training opportunities. If not, seek to have such a budget considered for the members of your team. Your church will benefit immeasurably by providing this opportunity for its pastors.

Presently the Pastor-Staff Leadership Department of the Baptist Sunday School Board offers the following Personal and Professional growth opportunities for pastors and pastoral team leaders:

The National Conference for Church Leadership
Church Program Training Center opportunities
Career Assessment and Personal Growth
Conferences through your State Convention and/or your Association
Professional resources for the growth and development of the leader

In addition to these and other Sunday School Board opportunities, countless seminars and conferences are offered by seminaries, colleges, churches, and other Christian organizations. Encourage your team members to find at least one of these events each year to attend. They will be enriched and your church will be blessed with a growing minister.

Encourage your team members to look at the five New Testament functions of *evangelism, discipleship, fellowship, ministry,* and *worship* and to determine personal and professional growth goals in each area. These become more meaningful and measurable to them and to the church when annual reviews are done each year. I heard of a church that had well-intentioned personnel committee members who used an annual review form from the local utility company to measure their staff's performance for the previous year. If we do not evaluate our team members with an instrument that mirrors our purpose statement, all comparisons are invalid and will fail to translate in any meaningful way that which God is doing in the lives of the individual team member.

Give your team the benefit of seeing your personal and professional growth goals in these five areas. Be sure to include your personal commitment to your family. Then ask your team members to write out their goals and give them to you in writing in a reasonable time frame (two weeks or less). Discuss the goals. Affirm them, or challenge them as may be appropriate. Pray with your team member about the identified goals. Pray for them on a regular basis. Encourage and affirm them when you see them doing something that gives evidence of their commitment to personal and professional growth. Your team members need to know that you not only expect them to grow, but that you will inspect their growth. Informally, they are already inspecting yours.

Ministry of Personal Relationships

Ministry requires our personal involvement with others. Jesus not only taught massive crowds, he also touched individuals, carried on private dialogues with people like Nicodemus, the woman at the well, visited in the home of Zacchaeus, and spent time with His disciples. He retreated for prayer on many occasions, but those times appear like bookends supporting entire volumes of personal touches and individual vignettes. Today's team member has many pressures. Society is fast paced. Cocooning is still a cultural reality. If our personal relationships are not tended, we will not recognize their absence and will wake up one day lonely and filled with the regret of what might have been.

As a team supervisor, you need to be a mirror to your team members, enabling them to see themselves more clearly. You may need to ask probing questions about some of the difficult relationships that you know exist in their ministry circles. At other times, you may be the key motivator to help your team members develop a support network of prayer partners. With the advent of the men's movement in full swing in our churches, the idea of accountability groups are at an all-time high. Encourage your team members to form a group if they have not already done so.

There are going to be times when you receive letters, phone calls, or in some other way learn that a team member is involved in a conflict resulting in an unreconciled relationship with a member of the congregation. The annual review is a time to help the team member (and the church) with a spiritual biopsy. Discuss the conflict. Review the damage and the potential destruction that will result if nothing is done to restore fellowship. Help the team member see the potential conflict as a satanic strategy bringing discord and brokenness into the life of the congregation. Establish a plan for reconciliation to begin.

Finally, help your team member see that the most important earthly relationship is with their family, especially if they are married and have children. One of my favorite pastors requires his team members to turn in a "time card" at their pastoral team meeting each week indicating the time spent with their families at night, away from church related activities. If more than 7 of the past 14 nights have involved church-related activities, that team member is violating the direction of the pastor by failing to develop their ministry of personal relationships at home. In a day when clergy couples are experiencing record divorce rates, this pastor sends a clear message to his team and his church about priorities. In turn, he not only is building a strong team, he is building a strong church. This kind of ministry often is *caught* more effectively than *taught.* When the church sees the importance placed on this ministry among team members, they begin to practice it as well.

Team Reports

Two final words of good advice. Document everything. Document the evaluation. Record the results of the performance review, changes needed to the ministry covenant or job description, all goals, both personal and professional, and document everything said regarding personal relationships. For one thing, you will be referring to this evaluation when you give your input to salary administration discussion in forthcoming budgets. You also will maintain a file on team members so that you can assist them with their growth goals throughout the year. Documentation will remind you to share a word of commendation following the significant achievement made by a team member.

INTERACTIVE QUESTIONS

"Mentoring is a relationship with someone you like, enjoy, believe in, and want to see win in life."[4]

If this definition is true, what kind of mentor are you?

____

Have you written your personal and professional growth goals for the present year? If so, have you asked your team members for their personal and professional growth goals?

____

When is the last time you invited your team to your home for a time of relaxing fellowship? What is keeping you from doing this if it has been a while? Are there any other options?

____

____

____

[1]Bobb Biehl, *Mentoring, Confidence in Finding a Mentor and Becoming One,* (Nashville: Broadman and Holman, 1996), 19.

[2]Ibid, 21.

[3]Doran McCarty, *Supervising Ministry Students,* (Atlanta, Home Mission Board of the SBC, 1986), 113.

[4]Ibid., 21.

CHAPTER 7

Building Team Strengths

In 1996, Tom Cruise thrilled many fans and won new admirers as he portrayed Ethan Hunt in a white-knuckling rendition of the 1960's super hit TV series, *Mission Impossible.* I did not see the movie, but I read the reviews. The special effects were stellar. The plot, even though difficult to follow at times, was a spellbinder. The familiar theme song, probably one of the most recognizable in the industry, did not disappoint. In spite of this, according to at least one review, something left record box-office crowds wanting. As stunning a performance as Tom Cruise delivered, he failed, or rather the plot failed, to accomplish the mission through *the work of a team.* Cruise makes Hunt the hero of the movie. Audiences who remember the original could not help but wonder where the IMF *team members* were.

Pastors who want to build great churches never forget the TEAM acrostic. Whether picked up in an Eagle Scout Summit, a church leadership seminar, a coach's locker-room speech before the second half, or lifted from the pages of an in-flight magazine, the words ring true. **TEAM: T**ogether **E**veryone **A**ccomplishes **M**ore. While it may not always be true in the movies, it is true in the plots of real life. We need each other.

If you are a senior pastor and you have others working beside you in professional ministry-leadership positions, you are challenged to turn them into a team. You may have inherited a "staff" or you may have been responsible for assembling one. Turn them into a team. Sometimes our interpersonal relationship skills, busy agendas, biased opinions shaded by past experiences, or even reasonable doubts in the present performance levels of others keep us from turning the staff on church letterheads into a team of the heart, but it is not impossible. Your mission, should you choose to accept it, is to be a team builder.

The following bulleted "quick list" is offered for the novice team builder as well as the seasoned veteran. These are basic reminders for some; epiphanal building blocks for others.

Minister to each member of your team. You will do this naturally when you pray for them daily. Look for ways to be the servant leader to your team. Wash their feet figuratively every opportunity you can. Visit them by dropping into their offices regularly just to chat. Minister to your team by practicing hospitality whenever you can (invite them into your home, or take them out for a surprise lunch). If you read a good book that ministers to you, chances are it will minister to them, too. Give them a copy and inscribe a note of appreciation inside the book jacket.

Minister to the family members of your team. They encounter more stringent expectations than any other member of the congregation, yet they are often "the forgotten parishioners in the church" (until help is needed in the pre-school department). If you do not regularly pray for them, begin today. If your team members are married, pray for the spouse and the marriage, and if they have children, mention each child by name.

Know when to use Extreme Pastoral Care. When a crisis comes into the family of a member of your team, the team builder gives what I call "extreme pastoral care." The shepherd/rancher motif is the model. While the senior pastor gives pastoral care in all situations in the local church to varying degrees, the multiplication of our ministry requires that we minister more intentionally to a group of leaders so that they can minister effectively to a growing church. One person cannot touch every life in the church effectively. Cases in point are the families of our pastoral team members. The ministry we provide to them in a time of need is critical. Be gracious. Give time off as is appropriate for the need. The ministry you provide in these times not only impacts their ability to deal with the crisis they are facing, it also shapes their future commitment to minister to the crisis needs of others.

Encourage your team members often. Church work is not always a place of encouragement. There are antagonists in almost every church. Sometimes, there are spiritual struggles. Loneliness and isolation characterize many ministries. In a recent survey, 40 percent of ministry spouses said that they would prefer that their spouse not choose to re-enter ministry professions if given an opportunity. This is an alarming reality. For one of the greatest callings God can place upon a life to be viewed in such contempt speaks to the need for more encouragement.

Affirm your team members weekly. In the weekly team meeting, tell the members of your team that they did a good job during the previous week. Recall the highlights of the past Sunday morning. Comment on how nice they looked, how well they represented Christ, how effective their ministry is, or how much you appreciate their faithfulness. If you look closely, you will find things to say that will affirm and strengthen team members' understanding of who they are in Christ. They have often heard how deficient they are. Human nature almost guarantees that they question their preparation many times. Do not underestimate the power of proper physical affirmation such as a pat on the back, strong eye-to-eye contact, a soft spoken and sincere word of appreciation, or even a written note.

Insist on personal mini-retreats. In multimember-team situations and in single-team-member churches, no one is so indispensable that a mini-retreat will stop the church dead in her tracks. Come on, who are we trying to fool! The church is not built on any one of us. To refresh your team members in a significant way, try letting one of them have a Sunday night or a Wednesday night off for a personal retreat.

The personal retreat is just what it says: it is personal. The team member can do anything they want to do. Some may stay home and relax with their family. Some may find a sitter and take off with their spouse for a long overdue get-away. The personal retreat is not vacation time. The personal retreat is not continuing education time. It is a time for the team member to retreat, change the pace briefly, spend some time renewing relationships with family or friends, or just rest. Jesus did this on occasion. We sometimes equate spirituality with burning the candle at both ends. This behavior is causing ministerial burnout and needs to cease. Team builders are willing to prioritize the mini-retreat.

Some nights are better than others. If you have the Singing Walendas coming in for a gospel sing-a-thon, consider letting one of your team members who has no responsibility in the evening program take the night as a mini-retreat. (Unless of course the Walenda thing was his idea, in which case you take a retreat!) If you have a mission program, a gospel film, a holiday weekend, or something similar, consider the value of letting one of your team members take the night as their retreat. Be fair. If you do it for one team member, do it for all during the course of the calendar year. Be sure to model it yourself! The moment you think you are indispensable is the moment you have passed the point of needing a mini-retreat: you need a therapist.

One effective way to model the value of the mini-retreat for the entire congregation is to look at the three official holiday weekends of the summer, Memorial Day, Independence Day, and Labor Day. One year our pastoral team recommended to the church that we should not have evening services on those three Sunday nights. Instead, they should be used as mini-retreats by members of the congregation. We told people to stay home, take a long nap on Sunday afternoon, eat out, relax, spend time with their children, and so forth. One grace-impaired person complained. The others had a tremendous night. Attendance on the other Sunday nights grew significantly in spite of the fact that it was "summer slump" time.

Take special days off. You can minister to your team members by giving them the opportunity to take special days off once in a while. Similar to the personal retreat, this is a personal day that you give them for the purpose of refreshing and refocusing, resting and renewing. If the spouse of a team member is a school teacher, a special day off might coincide with a school holiday. Team members will appreciate the opportunity to spend a day with their spouses during these special occasions. My experience is that team members are already putting in more hours than the average church member does in similar careers. In a day when ministry couples are having as much stress in their families as we are seeing, you are making an investment in the marriage of a team member by allowing them to observe this privilege. If their marriage suffers, their ministry will also suffer.

Commemorate special days. When a team member has a birthday, celebrate it. Taking the team member out to lunch with other members of the pastoral team can become a valued tradition. Gifts do not have to be given, but cards can be shared and the cost of the lunch can be divided among other members of the team. This provides a simple touch, but it becomes a fun tradition. If you can go to a restaurant in the community, invite the entire support team to go along, too. Find a volunteer to handle the phones for an hour so that you can be reached in an emergency, but enable the fellowship of the entire team to grow in these times of celebration. Let the church know about special days, too. Nothing substitutes for building a family atmosphere in the church like sharing the news of births, birthdays, wedding anniversaries, graduations, and special honors that relate to the membership of the congregation. This is especially true for members of the pastoral team. Many people in the church are looking for ways to express their love and appreciation. Enable them to do so by sharing the significant celebrations of our team members. In doing so, we build strength in the team as well as in the entire church fellowship.

Recognize ministerial competency. When records have been broken, commitments to Christ made, ministry performed, new classes started, pageants performed, or special recognitions given by denominational or community bodies, let the congregation know. Newsletter space and time following a worship service are well spent when we can recognize the accomplishments team members are making in the Kingdom.

Giving honor appropriately may minimize professional jealousies. There are individual and collective team strengths that need to be recognized. What one member of the team is able to accomplish due to their gift constellation and skill level will differ from what another team member can do. The evidence of individual accomplishments is often very obvious. When accomplishments are celebrated openly, the congregation is allowed to render a thank offering to the Lord for His faithfulness in supplying competent and called leadership to the congregation.

Giving recognition in these times can also provide spirited motivation. Everyone likes to be a part of a winning team. When the team is experiencing success, either individually or collectively, future successes are on the horizon. Momentum is a wonderful asset. Cultivate it by sharing the victories in an honest yet humble way. Thank God for His faithfulness, and recognize what He is doing through the efforts of your team.

Provide opportunities for growth and development. While I am a strong supporter of the mini-retreats mentioned in this chapter, nothing cultivates team building like professional development opportunities. In considering a budget for a new team member, it is imperative to plan for a salary that is the best the church can afford within a range commensurate with academic training and experience. In addition to this, program funds should be allocated for the ministry that you are calling a new team member to oversee. Often neglected are the funds that will enable a new team member to stay fresh mentally. Continuing education opportunities, leadership training, skill development, and personal enrichment opportunities will equip a team member for more effective service and ministry while enabling them to make a continued contribution to the effectiveness of the team. The church stands to benefit from making the investment in a minister's professional development.

Provide ministry tools and resources. There are numerous professional journals on the market designed to enhance the ministry of today's church leader. The Baptist Sunday School Board is committed to providing the best resources available anywhere to the leaders of our churches. Your team members will be strengthened and inspired each time they turn to these and other resources. Providing these tools is an inexpensive way to show a church's appreciation and support for a team member's ministry.

Be open to suggestions. Our team members have gifts and insights that are God-given. We usually benefit when we ask for suggestions because we multiply our eyes and ears. Your team members have risen to their level of expertise because they are good at what they do. Enable them to become collectively creative by asking them for suggestions when you face a difficult situation.

Laugh at yourself and with your team. The universal language of laughter has a bonding effect in our personal relationships. Holy humor is good medicine for the team (see Prov. 17:22).

Take your team out for desert following worship on a Sunday night. You do not need to do this every Sunday night, but the *regular fellowship* of your team and their families will build trust and appreciation for years to come. It also provides a ministry to those who see you fellowship as a team.

Send appropriate cards for birthdays and anniversaries. This can be a wonderful way of ministering to the team members and the family members of your team. Let them know that you appreciate them and are praying for them during the special days of their lives.

Use your influence with the appropriate committees at budget time. This is discussed in greater detail in other chapters of this book. However, your influence and presence as the leader during what are often tense days in the church are appreciated by the members of your team. They will see your integrity grow, and your willingness to care for them in a tangible way will not be forgotten.

Use "non-platform" team members once in awhile as "platform speakers." Some team members have responsibilities that often exclude them from worship leadership during most of the day on Sunday. Find ways to utilize them, even if briefly on occasion. Call them by name and highlight something special about their ministry. They will use different words and mannerisms in communicating than you do and in the process, they will broaden the scope of your ministry. Avoid putting team members in a rut by asking them to do the same thing over and over. (No one wants to be known as the Minister of Announcements throughout their entire career!) Let them pray, read Scripture, give a testimony, welcome the guests, participate in drama, sing, or use their spiritual gifts in ways that will edify the body. Let the church see them as a worship leader and a member of the team.

Call a coffee-break and require everyone to drop everything for ten minutes, especially during the week before major events when stress levels are high. This does not take long and will require very little preparation. My wife would bake lemon squares during these 'high-stress" times and bring them to the office. A short break can make almost any day seem less like "one of those days."

Let team members see their mistakes, but work quickly to resolve problems and move forward. I do not forget missed ministry opportunities. There are times when a hospital visit is never made. I've seen weeks go by when outreach visitation was not prioritized. Even the best pastoral teams are not perfect. Oversights are going to happen. Appointments are going to be forgotten. Policies are going to be violated. After having been confronted by a church member for my being insensitive when he experienced the death of an elderly non-immediate family member, I pulled the team together to discuss the issue. A plan emerged to enable us to provide better pastoral care in the future. We examined the mistake, tried to resolve the problem, and moved forward. Failure does not need to be met with a reprimand every time. Don't ignore mistakes, but don't send people to the firing squad either. Talk about what went wrong. Discuss how it could have been avoided. Develop a plan that will prevent the same thing from happening again. Inspect the plan once in a while. Move forward.

And finally, brethren, ***do everything you can to make your team members win.*** Following a loss to an across-town rivalry, a high-school basketball coach told his players not to worry about the loss of the game so long as they didn't lose the focus of basketball. "Basketball is something you use," he said. "When you let it use you, you lose." We have to let our team members see the church as a place to use our gifts and talents. When the church is seen using us, or worse, when a senior pastor is seen using the members of the team, everyone looses.

INTERACTIVE REFLECTION

The words listed below are action words that characterize some of the intentional actions of a team-building pastor. In what ways are you presently expressing these actions to the members of your team?

Nurture ____

Instruct ____

Affirm ____

Mentor ____

Model ____

Empower ____

Encourage ____

Uplift ____

Redeem ____

Build ____

Listen ____

In the space below, write the names of the members of your pastoral team. Beside their names, write one word from the list above that describes an action you need to intensify in your relationship with them.

____

____

____

____

CHAPTER 8

Weekly Team Meetings

If you are going to have a team, you must have a time when the team comes together for a team meeting. Once a week your team needs to have a formal meeting, complete with an agenda, driven by your purpose statement, underscored by prayer and a commitment to change the world. To do this requires planning.

You need to have weekly team meetings for several reasons. Secular businesses sometimes plan meetings around the fourfold objective, to inform, to train, to inspire, and to gain feedback.[1] The pastoral team of the local church must follow a slightly different agenda if it is going to be aggressive in fulfilling the church's purpose statement.

The ideal team meeting provides a climate where dreaming, sharpening, focusing, and planning are done in honesty and openness before ministerial peers. *Team meetings are the scheduled opportunities when the spiritual-gift mix that is unique to your team has the greatest possibility of yielding itself as an offering to the sovereignty of God.* When your team comes together, does this last thought ever enter anyone's mind?

Probably not, at least not all the time. Realistically, team meetings have become necessary "church maintenance evils" or "crisis intervention sessions" where we show less than our best relational skills to those called to minister beside us. These weekly meetings have been known to be times when the senior leader acts like anything but a senior leader. It's possible that if the environment of our weekly meetings were to change, those with whom we minister might become more "team-like" in the process.

The Basics of the Team Meeting

Timing. Team meetings need to take place often enough to give passionate impetus to the fulfilling of the church purpose statement. This frequency also serves to refine the individual commitments of team members to their specific responsibilities within that purpose statement. Once a week is probably best for most teams in most churches. This provides the opportunity for weekly evaluation to take place as well as effective management of work loads and ministry responses.

My preference is to make Monday the administration day of my week, scheduling team meetings on Monday mornings from 9:00 to 11:30. Planning the team meeting agenda requires taking notes during the previous week and processing them into an agenda on Monday morning. Mornings normally work best for these meetings. Afternoons tend to give way to somnambulistic slumber following the lunch hour, if not half-a-dozen post-Sunday emergencies. Furthermore, Monday afternoon is the perfect time to follow through on most of the team assignments that will be generated during the weekly team meeting.

Location. Space often requires that team meetings take place in the team leader's office or study. Some teams have the luxury of using a conference room. Since this is a formal meeting, public places such as restaurants are not encouraged. Use those locations for special meetings, but not for the weekly team meeting. The room needs to be large enough for those in attendance to have a comfortable place to work. Seating, lighting, and other facility concerns should be considered.

Attendance. Since it is important for the *entire team* to function as a unit, I encourage every member of the pastoral team and the immediate support team to attend the first few minutes of the team meeting. The professional support team includes the administrative assistants, secretaries, and receptionists. Someone may need to stay close to the phone during this time in most churches, so a rotating system is encouraged that will allow everyone on the team to participate at least marginally. Following the fellowship time and the team devotion and prayer time, the support team return to their stations, leaving only the office coordinator and the pastoral team in the meeting. Following the time in which calendar issues are addressed, the office coordinator can be effectively dismissed. The members of the pastoral team remain at this point to deal with pastoral leadership issues in the team meeting.

Some Interesting Contrasts

The agendas for the task-oriented team meetings are impersonal, result driven, and guilt motivated. The agenda for the team-building meeting are relational, purpose driven, and grace motivated. The task-oriented leader uses "you" and "yours" in his meetings, usually to underscore deficiency and disappointment. The team builder uses "we" and "ours," eliciting team ownership and encouraging member accountability. Task-oriented agendas have deadlines; team-building agendas have celebrations. Task-oriented agendas work well in Fortune 500 board rooms run by CEO's with MBA's. Team-building agendas would more easily be used on grassy hillsides, carpentry shops, or wherever fishermen repair their nets.

If you need a model, try the three-component agenda described in the following pages. (A manipulatable text outline is found in this resource on the floppy disk.) The team-building leader of a growing church needs an agenda that will enable him to lead a church to: (1) build the team, (2) reach the community, and (3) minister to the body.

Building the Team

Building the team is a process that happens over a period of time. Team builders have to develop certain skills, and they have to draw certain characteristics out of team members in order for team-building to be realized. The team meeting is one of the most crucial places for this to happen, because it is our only formal arena for defining who we are as ministers outside that of worship leadership.

The ministers who co-labor with you on your team are people. Because of this, they have some of the same needs as the people to whom you seek to minister. They need to be encouraged. They need to be appreciated. They need to know that others are genuinely concerned about them. At times they need shepherd-like correction. With plethoric personal investments, all of which stretch them emotionally, physically, and spiritually, they need to know that someone is interested in them. The team-building leader not only understands this; he intentionally plans for it. There are many ways to express this understanding in any given week in the local church, but nothing gives the formal recognition of this in the same way as the team meeting.

Task-oriented leaders are not going to be concerned with the building of the team beyond the point that the team makes them look good. Because of this, when their reflection is viewed critically, the leader uses guilt, fear, manipulation, and other positional leadership resources in an attempt to bring something more tangibly measurable out of the members comprising the team. This works temporarily in some cases, but more often than not eventually results in the displacing of team members, or the grind of a dysfunctional teamwork environment.

Building the team through fellowship. You will build team spirit by beginning your team meetings with an informal time of fellowship. Team members genuinely enjoy spending time together planning and working. Your team will learn to be committed to the discipline of fellowship and will want to interact closely with one another. A time to laugh together or catch up on personal issues is a valuable prelude to a productive meeting. Using simple relational skills, the team-building leader engages members of the team, or joins in the conversations of team members setting the tone for everything that is going to happen in the meeting. A simple comment or statement of affirmation to a member of the team regarding a celebrative victory realized during the previous week is sometimes all that is needed to establish an open and winning atmosphere.

Team building through spiritual nurture. It is natural to see this time of fellowship yield itself to a time of devotion and prayer. The team-building leader may deliberately choose to lead in this time. The devotion may be a time of training, inspiring, informing, mentoring, correcting or encouraging. Being led by the Spirit of God, the team builder feels as strong about nurturing the team during these moments as he does about feeding the entire congregation on a Sunday morning.

Having a fresh word from the Lord requires additional study and preparation. Devotions may come from the overflow of the leader's private worship patterns. Such team-intensive content probably requires that he be additionally well read in order to address the issues in a relevant and inspiring manner. Included in *The Team Builder* material is a 3.5" computer disk containing 52 encouraging team-intensive devotions. These are intended for your use in leading and guiding your team during the devotional time of your team meetings.

The devotion time ends in prayer for the specific application of the insights gained in the devotion. Team members should be encouraged to share personal prayer needs that they have prior to the devotional message so that upon its conclusion, the team can be encouraged to deal with the content of the devotion by responding to the Holy Spirit with no further distraction.

A good practice would be to begin this time by asking a member of the team to write down the prayer needs as they are shared and to be prepared to lead in prayer for them following the devotion. At times, it may be very helpful to enlist team members to lead the devotion. This gives them the opportunity of growing and expanding their gifts in a unique environment. What they will share will not only challenge the team, it will further knit the team together by developing leaders. The team builder will be blessed as team members share, and he will be better able to assess the spiritual maturity of the individual team members.

The devotion time has a tendency to become a time consuming part of the team meeting. While we do not want to hinder the work of the Holy Spirit, we need to set an example of brevity and encourage this same sensitivity upon enlisting team members to share devotional messages. Some teams experience team meetings that exceed two and three hours in length. For these teams, the devotion includes accountability reports and extended prayer time. The issue is not meeting length, but meeting content. If you are attempting team meetings with no time of reflection and prayer, you are missing out on a rich time of spiritual growth needed by your leaders. For team meetings that will last, on average, two hours, a twenty-minute time of fellowship and devotion seems adequate.

Building the team through corporate time disciplines. Another feature of the team-building portion of the team meeting needs to be the discipline of corporate time management. Following the fellowship and devotional part of your team meeting, you may want to dismiss all the support team members, with the exception of the member who carries most of the office manager responsibilities. This is a great time to review the church calendar and to identify short-term and long-range projects on the horizon. Personal calendar dates can be discussed as necessary during this time. Scheduling room availability and meeting times can prevent team conflicts as ministry plans are made. Following this, the office coordinator can be dismissed.

Personal issues relative to the team. Occasionally there may be matters of sensitive personal content that need to be discussed in this time dedicated to building the team. Deal with them at this point if they are team issues. If they are individual-leadership issues, you should choose to deal with them at another time. An example of a team issue might be a personnel policy decision, a strategy for dealing with spiritual antagonism in the body, or the resolution of a conflict in the church. Individual leadership issues, possibly dealing with team-member disciplinary actions, an evaluation, or even an accusation against a team member need to be handled with more discretion and grace for obvious reasons.

REACHING THE COMMUNITY

Because evangelism and missions were such high priorities in my church, we immediately moved from the team-building portion of our meeting to a time when we focused on reaching our community. As a matter of agenda concern, this both practically and philosophically stressed the priority that was placed upon our commitment to evangelism. Whatever occupies such a high profile position on your team meeting agenda will eventually drive your commitments in ministry.

Formal accountability. I did not hesitate to ask our team members about their personal involvement in evangelism by asking them to report on the contacts they had made during the previous week. This formal accountability is a requirement if you are going to lead your church in fulfilling the great commission. I usually began this section of our team meeting by sharing the names of the people I had witnessed to or visited in the previous week. Then I would ask, "Who's next?" Without fail, everyone said something. Some reported the results of their visitation assignments; some told of the frustration they were having in finding anyone home during the previous week. Everyone said something without guilt or ministerial exaggeration. We all had weeks characterized by frustration once in a while. The honesty of this kind of accountability encouraged lifestyle evangelism. My team members shared Christ because they wanted to, not because they had a quota. Because they were nurtured and encouraged in this way, they usually surpassed most of the quotas used by my task-oriented counterparts.

Something natural grew out of this. First, the members of my team knew that I was involved in this vital ministry because of my example. Second, they knew that personal involvement was expected of them. The third result contributed to team building like nothing else. If a team member had been instrumental in leading an individual to Christ, we celebrated that victory during the team meeting. In the following weeks, when that person came forward to follow Christ in baptism or unite with our church, I would be sure to mention the pastor's name who ministered to them before the entire church. In this way, the congregation constantly saw the value in their pastoral team. (I also shared the same information if a lay-member of the church was involved.) A special bond is created among the team members and in the church when this affirmation is repeated. God gets the glory; we simply get to be a part of the process.

First-Time Worshipers (FTW's). Following the report time in team meetings, our attention would be given to the first-time worshipers from one of the five worship services of the previous week. Our method for doing this evolved over the years but basically followed this procedure:

First-time worshipers were asked to complete an information card during worship on Sundays. These cards were placed in the offering plate as the first-time worshipers' "offering" during the time of worship. Ushers took the cards out of the offering plates and left them on the desk of the pastor responsible for outreach and assimilation. On Monday mornings, the first priority of his support team was to enter the information on each card into our outreach database. A printed sheet listing all pertinent information from each card was prepared for each pastoral team member prior to our team meetings.

As we began this second phase of our team meeting the pastor responsible for follow-up walked us through the list of names. This was an important time for us because it reinforced the names and faces (or other identifiable characteristics) of first-time worshipers in our minds. We might have picked up something in a casual conversation with a first-time worshiper that could help us assimilate them more effectively into the life of our church. For example, if a person expressed interest in a specific ministry, we could assign someone involved in that ministry to contact them. If that same first-time worshiper indicated a religious heritage that a member in our congregation formerly embraced, we might want to include them in the visitation assignment.

Our congregation shared in the responsibility of making personal contacts with each first-time worshiper so it was not the responsibility of the pastoral team to see everyone on our list each week. However, it was a responsibility of each member of our pastoral team to see someone on the list each week. During the team meetings, the pastoral team got "first choice" of who they were going to see that week in their personal outreach ministry.

Brainstorm. We also used this time in our meetings to brainstorm our entire evangelistic strategy. Special events would be discussed and planned that would involve our church in an ongoing commitment to reach the unreached in our community. At times, this would spill into discussions regarding our investment in missions, locally and internationally. At other times we would plan our next mass-mail campaign.

Ministering to the Body

Growing churches can fall prey to the unfair accusation that all the pastoral team thinks about are numbers. Because there is sometimes truth in this evaluation, we designed our team-meeting agenda with the third section concerning the church family. Ministering to the body is an essential requirement for building a balanced and healthy church. This portion of our team meeting was characteristically longer than others.

One of the first items on the agenda in this section involved evaluation. We evaluated everything we did, often erring on the side of ruthless criticism. We would bring the printed worship guide into our evaluations of worship. Nothing was sacred, including the welcome and announcements, solos, congregational singing, instrumentals, the choir anthem, the sermon, the invitation, and the benediction. We evaluated the technical aspects, including lighting, sound, extra seating, and building temperature. This environment enabled our team to sharpen the effectiveness of everything we did. It also helped us in planning for ways to be more effective in the future. While the pastor responsible for the music ministry would meet with me at other times in the week for worship planning, having input from the other pastors was very helpful.

Ministering to the body also includes ministering to the physical needs of those in the congregation as well. We sought to maintain a list of those anticipating hospitalization so that, each week, hospital visitation could be planned. This elementary discipline of pastoral care cannot be overlooked nor completely delegated to a ministry team composed of the laity. Growing churches have to address this important role of ministry and make appropriate decisions regarding team responsibility.

Similarly, pastoral team involvement must be provided for the institutionalized and immobilized. Providing pastoral care for members of the body who are in nursing homes, correctional facilities, or simply confined to the home is a time consuming part of ministry. While the membership of the congregation can be trained and encouraged to participate in this task, often ministering more capably than we due to their gifts and passions, we can make indelible impressions for the cause of Christ by being sensitive with timely cards, calls, and brief visits (even at church) with the family members dealing with these life transitions. Our team meetings were always a time to report on and be sensitive to these ministry needs.

It was not always this intentional. We learned to become sensitive the hard way by letting some significant ministry opportunities slip through the cracks. It does not take many of those to learn the importance of a timely note, a floral arrangement, a phone call, or a personal visit. The effort and expense of this intentional response will pay dividends far into the future.

Team meetings enabled us to address these important ministry opportunities and to become familiar with the circumstances surrounding the member. When we made ministry contacts we could raise genuine questions of concern or make comments that would let the member know he or she had been in our thoughts and prayers.

Ministering to the body also included strategic planning. During this section of our meeting, we attempted to address both the discovered and anticipated needs of our congregation for training, equipping, development, and encouragement in the five functional areas of the church: evangelism, discipleship, fellowship, ministry and worship.[2] This strategic planning provided balance in our ministry plans and enabled us to be driven by our purpose statement instead of the urgent crises that characterize ministry.

Other Items

The final section of our agenda became a "catchall" for anything needing attention that had been inadvertently omitted from the agenda. "Other Items" provides an opportunity for input from members of the team. This communicates that they are important as contributing members of the team. As team building becomes more natural, the items added at this point will become fewer because the leader has given careful thought to the development of the team meeting and has been thorough in providing the leadership necessary to cover individual concerns.

The following is a sample of a printed agenda used in team meetings.

Pastoral Team Meeting

February 22, 1998

Agenda

- Building the Team

- Fellowship

- Devotion

- Prayer Time

- Calendar Issues

- Reaching the Community
  Reports from the Week of February 16
  FTW's from Sunday, February 21
  Silverado Mission
    Music needs
    Leadership retreat
    More chairs for Easter Service

- Ministering to the Body

- Sunday's Evaluation

- LIFELines (Newsletter Content Planning)

- 48 Hour Prayer Vigil

- Hospital Concerns
  John Floyd (by-pass surgery Feb. 24, Sunrise Hospital)
  Ginny Masterson (girl, St. Francis Hospital)

- Discovered Needs
  - Evangelism
    - Fourth Annual People Sharing Jesus Seminar
    - NAMB Missions Offering Goal
    - More prayer partners needed for decision time
  - Discipleship
    - More space needed for Communication and Intimacy Class
    - Status of Preschool One teacher
  - Fellowship
    - Fox Ridge Park reservation for May 28
    - New Member's Banquet, April 13
  - Ministry
    - Team Ministry Training, March 15, 7:00
    - Youth Evangelism Team needs budget increased
  - Worship
    - Lord's Supper service during Holy Week

- Other Items

Characteristics of Effective Team Meetings

We've all seen lists of the important things that characterize effective meetings. Giving attention to the administrative details of planning a meeting is important for team builders and team members. For example, meetings should begin and end on time; agendas should be available prior to the meeting so that members will be prepared to participate; audio-visuals, handouts, overheads, and such should be prepared and ready for distribution; and so on. Team builders may turn to an inexhaustible resource for these elements in any good library or church administration handbook.

The following go beyond the basics and comprise the commitments that are going to be necessary for effective team meetings needed in our churches today.

Effective team meetings are conducted in an attitude of absolute dependency upon the Holy Spirit of God. We've operated in the flesh for far too long. Mere talented leadership will never meet the future demands our churches will face if God sends revival. Only that leadership which recognizes the complete ineffectiveness of the flesh will be able to experience what only God wants to accomplish through the church. The effective team meeting is a gathering of spiritually gifted individuals committed to seeing God use them in extraordinary ways.

Effective team meetings are led by a mentoring visionary who consistently demonstrates servant leadership. When we build teams, we are making long-lasting investments in the ministry of our churches for tomorrow. Like championship coaches, team builders are investors. They have learned the value of multiplying themselves through others. Their meeting agendas are derived from a deep well of personal contentment in Christ that has made them accustomed to exemplary roles of surrendered servanthood. It is who they are as surrendered persons under the lordship of Christ. Effective team meetings have their hearts' fingerprints all over them.

Effective team meetings have a prayerfully stated agenda that is consistent with the purpose statement of the church. Since fewer than four percent of the pastors in a recent survey could articulate a clear vision for their ministry,[3] it is no wonder that weekly team meetings seem to accomplish so little for the kingdom of God. Effective team meetings are guided by agendas harvested out of an understanding of why the church is in business in the first place. They are not strategy meetings called in reaction to worldly pressure, nor are they flagrant antagonism. They are meetings that position the people of God to change the world.

Effective team meetings affirm the gifts and reinforce the individual value of every member on the team. Team-building leaders recognize the spiritual giftedness found in others and respond to ministry needs by positioning gifted team members to be used and developed. Team members are not only in attendance and accounted for, they make valuable contributions to that which God has called the church to accomplish in her unique ministry setting. Members of the team eagerly anticipate the next team meeting because they are passionate about their gifts and calling, and cannot wait to see how God is going to involve them in meeting future challenges faced by the body.

Effective team meetings provide an exclusive ministry to members of the team that can not be accomplished any other way. God's Word promises that every time members of the body come together, the Lord is present. This is equally true for the times when the pastoral team comes together. The effective team meeting ministers to the individual team member in a way that no other meeting can because of the presence of the Lord found in that unique gathering of ministerial professionals. It is a time of iron sharpening iron—not always pleasant, but always potentially valuable.

---

[1] Dun & Bradstreet Business Library, *How to Conduct a Meeting* (New York: Thomas Y. Crowell Company, 1969).

[2] Eugene Mims, *Kingdom Principles for Church Growth* (Nashville: Convention Press, 1994).

[3] George Barna, *Today's Pastors* (Ventura, Calif.: Regal Books, 1993), 118.

INTERACTIVE APPLICATION

If you use a formal agenda in your team meetings, change it for the next several meetings, using the three-component design recommended in this chapter. You will find a customizable text file on the disk accompanying this resource to make the agenda more accessible. You will find devotional ideas on the same disk arranged by month and week. Some devotions are usable anytime; others are calendar sensitive (December/Christmas).

After using the new agenda for several weeks, what feedback are you receiving from your team that may be helpful in the development of an agenda outline that suits your needs better?

____

____

____

____

____

____

Review the Five Characteristics of Effective Team Meetings. Which ones are new to your way of thinking? How will they affect the way in which you plan your next team meeting?

____

____

____

____

____

CHAPTER 9

How to Do Long-Range Planning As a Pastoral Team

Where there is no vision, the people perish. (Prov. 29:18)

Unapologetically, I am absolutely convicted that a New Testament church has one basic model. *The church is to be Holy Spirit empowered, pastor led, deacon served, and lay ministered* (to make a verb out of a noun as it seems intended.) Within this model there will be variations regarding the kinds of ministry, but the model must not become corrupt. A corrupt model would be for the deacons to empower the pastors to serve the laity hoping that the Holy Spirit will minister.

You honestly can't blame an existing church for being a little nervous about the reins of leadership. Most churches have had three senior pastors in the last three years. Each one came and interpreted a vision for the church. Faithfully, some of those churches rearranged their pews, bulletins, and their finances to see the new vision unfold. When the senior leader came to the end of his vision and left, the church had to start over. If you have come along following some of those myopic visionaries, don't expect a standing ovation when you preach your best "I have a Dream" sermon. Chances are, the people already have whiplash from turning their heads and adjusting their vision one too many times.

Still, I am convinced. *Long-range planning is a process that should be led by the pastoral team, not a committee.* It goes through the process model of *Kingdom Principles Growth Strategies* and is fleshed out by the leadership structure of the local church, but it is led by the pastoral team. Using *Kingdom Principles Growth Strategies*, a church can do a five-year plan and evaluate it annually. The pastoral team evaluates it weekly in team meetings and quarterly in strategic planning meetings.

Church leaders may help pastoral teams shape the long-range plan, but it is born and nurtured in the vision for ministry that God has put within the heart of the pastors of His churches. The team-building pastor is going to be willing to invest years of his life into the ministry of the church in order to become its leader. When this is accomplished, he will emerge not only as the trusted leader, but also as the anticipated visionary. You do not become a leader by accepting a call. In many cases, that may be anticipated and it may even be in the job description, but becoming a leader takes time. I know these things about leadership and vision:

1. The leader must have a vision.
2. The leader must be able to communicate the vision.
3. The leader must be able to help others see the vision.
4. The leader has to know when to move toward the vision.

Even so, there are things that can be done by every pastoral team in the Kingdom that will enable them to lead the church to see their vision in perhaps an accelerated manner as the one who influences ministry or the long-range planner. None of these things begins with a calendar nor a business meeting. These things begin in a prayerful understanding of the church's purpose.

Developing Purpose and Vision Statements

It is unfathomable today for a church to have no purpose statement. If no one in your church knows why you are in business, what it is that is unique about your business, and how you intend to carry on your business, you probably are out of business. Years ago I heard a chapel speaker in seminary make the statement that the church exists in order to do what Jesus would do if He were here in person. Dr. Gene Mims has reminded the church that we are about Kingdom business and states that business as the one driving force of the church which is summed up in the Great Commission passage, Matthew 28:19-20 *(Kingdom Principles for Church Growth).*

Purpose Statement

From a pastor's personal and prayerful study of the Great Commission, a purpose statement needs to emerge. This statement needs to be a carefully worded statement that is easy to remember. The purpose statement needs to be specific. *The purpose statement clarifies and explains what the church is.* The wise team builder will review this statement with the members of his team so that they can prayerfully assist him in refining it. In confidence, the team builder will discuss the statement with his trusted prayer supporters and again, ask them for suggestions that will help him arrive at a clear, understandable, defensible sentence.

Vision Statement

Following this, the team builder brings his team together and begins to "flesh out" the purpose statement. What Dr. Mims calls a vision statement in *Kingdom Principles Growth Strategies* is simply a way of saying what the church does because of who the church is. *Vision statements grow out of our understanding of the Great Commission as action statements explaining how we do the work of the church.*

The pastoral team works on the attending vision statements until they are succinct and ready for further development. The vision statements help the pastoral-team members envision ministry strategies. Long-range planning is difficult if we simply equate it with calendaring event after event on a church calendar. When it becomes an incarnational reality, the passions of the team begin to rise to the surface. This process takes time. Do not expect to accomplish all of this in one quick weekend getaway. Prayer and continual sharpening of the statements will impact the process, and these must have a gestational period unless you are accustomed to getting inscribed tablets from the tops of mountains every three years.

Dr. Mims developed the "Growth Strategies Map" in his book *Kingdom Principles for Church Growth*. If a pastoral team follows the map, they will have the necessary perspective to begin long-range or strategic planning. The map takes into consideration the spiritual giftedness of the congregation, the needs discovered in the church's community, and the assimilation of these under the headings of Strengths, Weaknesses, Opportunities, and Threats.

Many churches play to their strengths. They have done this for years. The problem is that by continually playing to your strengths, you fail to respond to the threats found all around you. When left unattended, these threats eventually will appear stronger than the identifiable strengths. You can pretend to do long-range planning, but if your plan does not address the opportunities and threats, it is only a short-range plan at best.

Setting Goals

Often, long-range planning consists of arbitrary exercises of setting goals. *Kingdom Principles Growth Strategies* will make long-range planning a much more meaningful exercise. Taking the five functions of *evangelism, discipleship, ministry, fellowship,* and *worship,* the pastoral team responds to the threats and opportunities by *prioritizing new ministry possibilities.*

These become the basis for long-range planning, not numbers. Let God worry about the numbers. The pastoral team's responsibility is to respond to the needs that are discovered in a prayerful process of seeing the church and the community through the lenses of the Great Commission.

If you have assembled or inherited a team, no doubt some of them have the ability to evaluate the resources needed for the prioritized ministries uncovered in the process. A pastor with religious education responsibilities will be able to analyze the man hours, space, and training needs that will be created as well as many of the potential impacts these new ministry priorities will have on people and church finances. If you are pastoring a single-member pastoral-team church, find a competent layman to assist you with these issues, or ask a respected and trained worker to assist you from another church in your area or your state or regional denominational support agency such as a Baptist convention office.

Now That I've Begun, What's Next?

Assuming that you have developed a Purpose Statement and the attending Vision Statements following a study of the Great Commission, share this with your pastoral team. Resist the urge to preach your vision at this point. Simply hold it close to your chest for a few weeks, allowing it to mature and develop.

You may schedule a one-day Pastoral-Team Retreat for the purpose of refining the statements. Encourage the members of your team to share ideas for implementation of the vision statements, but do not put them in stone yet.

You will need the support of your church leadership. This may include a body of deacons, a Church Council, or even an unofficial group of spiritual leaders the Lord has provided for you. In every presentation, anticipate both positive and negative feedback. You are still refining (not changing) at this point. Approach these groups as valued, prayer-support groups. When formulating something as potentially impacting as a long-range planning strategy, you will need all the prayer support you can get.

Inform these groups that you will be sharing the results of your study on the Great Commission soon. Ask them to pray with you about that sermon and the ones to follow that are intended to prepare your church for the strategies that are being considered. A suggested idea is to preach a sermon on each of the five functions identified in *Kingdom Principles for Church Growth.*

Continue meeting with your pastoral team to develop a Vision Report. This ministry plan should address the issues discovered in your development of the ministry priorities. At this point, you will begin formalizing a calendar, not only to make time commitments, but also as a way of placing the vision before your congregation.

The planning phase solidifies when a ministry budget is prepared that will support the ministry plans. Action plans are completed. It is now time for the church to hear from its leaders.

No plan is complete in the local church until it has received church body acceptance and ownership. This requires the communication of the vision which will be done in numerous ways.

- Preaching and worship plans
- Letters from the pastor
- Testimonies from church leaders
- Presentations from the members of the pastoral team

and affirmed by the Holy Spirit in times of prayer and searching.

It is significant in the minds of our people that they be able to express their personal commitment to the Lord by affirming the ministry plans with a show of support. While I do not believe in a "democratic" form of government for the church, which is not biblical, I do believe that a congregation should be encouraged to prayerfully seek the heart of God in a matter and then express their commitment accordingly. Once this is done, the church has much to celebrate.

Some call this process "Team Initiated Ministry," which is a good term for a biblically based idea for ministry. Such a process enables gifted and trained pastors to do what they do best in addressing the needs and ministry concerns of their area of expertise. Then, the process continues by enabling lay leaders to sharpen the vision for ministry that God is giving to the entire church.

Kingdom Principles Impact Everything

By using the process model found in *Kingdom Principles for Church Growth,* everything a church does will be impacted.

Budget Planning. The church budget is organized around the five New Testament functions, and nothing is placed in the church budget that does not relate to the five New Testament functions of the Church.

Ministry Teams. Following the "Ministry Gifts Inventory" that is a part of *Kingdom Principles Growth Strategies,* church members are encouraged to join ministry teams and put their spiritual gifts to work. Deacon leaders of the ministry teams provide the accountability and ministry encouragement needed to keep people ministering.

Weekly Team Meetings. Weekly team-meeting agendas are designed around the five New Testament Functions of the Church. As each category is reviewed by members of the pastoral team balance is encouraged in the ministry of the church.

Team-Member Evaluations. Upon their call to the church, members of the pastoral team are asked to set personal and professional goals in the areas relative to the five New Testament functions. During their annual reviews with the appropriate supervisor, each growth goal is evaluated in the team member's life. Pastoral team members are encouraged to do self evaluation in this process. This enables performance reviews to relate specifically to the purpose statement of the church. Evaluations become more meaningful and measurable for the team members and the church family.

Administration. Using *Kingdom Principles Growth Strategies* as designed enables a church to prioritize ministry. As a church resources to achieve the ministry plans birthed in long-range planning, all administrative details are limited to the support of the growth strategy.

Calendaring. The discipline of corporate time management must not be overlooked. Preparing a ministry calendar that is prioritized by the growth plans established in the Kingdom Principles process enables a church to focus its resources on that which is most important. Nothing that is not directly related to the five New Testament functions needs to hinder a church from fulfilling her purpose.

Ministry Resources. When churches make deliberate attempts to prioritize the five New Testament functions, they make better uses of the resources of time, space, people, finances and trained leadership. Ministry intensive churches are healthy churches, and they are led courageously by team builders!

What Are the Advantages?

The process calls for a leader to come before God seeking the vision that God has for the church. This is foundational to our future; thus, it has every imaginable advantage over goals and numbers that are at best humanly contrived. No one has to climb and preach from the roof of the building, but they will have to find the heart of God, and this can only be done in humble prayer and private worship. The psalmist said it best:

> *Except the Lord build the house, they labour in vain that build it: except the Lord keep the city, the watchman waketh but in vain. (Ps. 127:1)*

INTERACTIVE REFLECTION

Does your church have a purpose statement? Can you write it down without looking at it?

____

____

____

If someone asked the average member of your church to give them the purpose statement of the church, what do you think they would say?

____

____

____

Someone recently said that a church that has business meetings monthly probably does not have a purpose statement. If a guest attended your church for the first time during a business meeting, what would they know about your church from that first impression?

____

____

____

What are you leading your pastoral team to do about any of the issues raised here?

____

____

____

CHAPTER 10

Refreshing the Team Spirit

When your car begins to run "sluggishly" it might need a tune-up. Chances are, it does not need to be replaced. Think of all the similarities between a car that is "sluggish" and a pastoral team needing a good retreat. The car may seem sluggish until you upgrade the gasoline, add a little oil, give it a good wash and wax, change the air in the tires, put in a new set of spark plugs, or even "open her up and blow her out" on the freeway once. You may even need a real tune-up. When the team seems sluggish, a retreat may be the equivalent of a tune-up.

Look at the "stuff" team members often deal with in an average year in the local church.

- 12 deacons meetings
- 12 board or council meetings
- 50 Pastoral Team Meetings
- 52 Sundays to staff the preschool extended care, secure soloists, or replenish toilet paper supplies
- 1 week of Vacation Bible School
- 1 revival or similar event
- 12 weddings
- 12 funerals
- 3 musical pageants
- One full-length drama presentation
- One youth camp
- One children's camp
- One stewardship campaign
- One singles retreat
- 36 Sunday School class fellowships
- 10 invitations for dinner

- 5 or more crisis situations regarding marriages, teenagers, immorality, or drugs

Add to these events the individual ministry that is conducted by the average minister in a given year such as …

- 150 worship services to plan and conduct
- 100 counseling sessions (of which over half of them he is not qualified to assist)
- 10 antagonistic encounters with church members
- 10 meetings involving denominational responsibilities
- 10 prayer breakfast meetings
- 50 hospital visits
- 50 visits to the homes of prospective members
- 300 phone calls regarding everything from "what is so-and-so's phone number?" to "what time are we supposed to be there?" questions
- 5 visits from copy machine, telephone, fax, janitorial supplies, and fund-raising salesmen

Not only is it a wonder we ever get anything done, it is a wonder we do not go crazy in the process and look for something else to do with our lives. The wise team builder knows this and recognizes *the importance of planning a team retreat.*

Planning

Team retreats can be wonderful experiences … or they can be nightmares. It depends on how well the basics of planning are conducted by the team builder. Once you have determined that a retreat is needed and you have in your mind what you want the retreat to accomplish, you are ready to begin planning the details. A retreat purpose and a retreat theme are essential.

Be "achievement-motivated" as you plan this time of refreshment. The purpose of the retreat needs to be defensible. Know what you want to accomplish and why. Retreat achievements may be:

- To refresh the spirit of the pastoral team by establishing new goals for ministry and personal development.
- To strengthen the fellowship capacity of members of the pastoral team by focusing on the ministry of personal relationships.
- To identify team weaknesses and develop strategies for compen-

sating for them.

- To refocus the team's attention on the Kingdom principles for church growth, and the impact of those principles in facing the new millennium.

Like a purpose statement for a church, *a retreat needs to have a purpose statement.* We are asking the members of our team to give us their time and personal energies. We also are asking the church to make a considerable investment of finances and trust. The planning must be exceptional.

Once you have the purpose statement written, begin your "blue sky" planning process by asking the following questions:

- In addition to the members of the pastoral team, who (if anyone) needs to be present and for how long?
- Where would the most effective and practical retreat setting be for this team retreat?
- Who would be best at challenging or training this team in order to move us toward the specific achievements identified?
- What resources will be needed to assist the team in achieving the goals of the retreat?
- What are some ways I can show my appreciation (and if appropriate, that of the congregation's) for the members of this team while on this retreat?

Determine the answers to these questions, and then proceed to the cost planning process of this retreat.

Since it is somewhat common in many churches for the lay leaders to be familiar with the value and expectations for professional development in the secular society, requesting the underwriting for a team retreat may be the easiest part of the planning process. In other churches, the mentality may be somewhat different. In either case, a well-thought-out plan presented by an achievement motivated leader will be appreciated and should aid in the shared ownership required for the success of the team retreat. A Retreat Planning Form similar to the one shown in this chapter should enable the team-building pastor to present the cost planning information to the appropriate individuals for consideration and approval. (The form also can be found on the computer diskette that accompanies this resource.)

Team Retreat Expense Planning Form

Team Retreat Target Date:_______________________

TRAVEL BUDGET: (Anticipated expenses for travel to the retreat setting)

- *Airfare:* _____________ per round trip ticket, for _________ Team Members = _____________ .
- *Rental Car(s):* ____________ cars at _______________ per day, for _________ days = ____________ .
- *Mileage for Use of Personal Vehicle:* ________ miles at .31 per mile for __________ cars = ____________ .
- *Parking (at the airport, or at the retreat setting):* _____________ cars at ____________ per day, for _________ days = _____________ .
- *Gasoline for rental cars:* _______________
- *Other:* ____

(Estimated Travel Total) ______________________________________.

ACCOMMODATIONS

- *Single Room Occupancy Rates:* ____________ rooms, ________ nights.
- *Meeting Room and Breaks (if applicable):* ___________________.

(Estimated Accommodation Total) ___________________________.

MEALS: Calculate the expenses of each meal, multiply that meal by the number of team members anticipated, enter the total in each cell.

	Day One	Day Two	Day Three	Totals
Breakfast				
Lunch				
Dinner				
Totals				

(Estimated Meals Total) ______________________________________.

TEAM BUILDING EXERCISES

(Estimated Total) ____.

RETREAT PASTOR HONORARIUM ________________________.

(Total Pastor/Facilitator Expenses Estimated) ___________________.

RETREAT MATERIALS (for Training, Planning, Research, Evaluating)
(Total Estimated Materials) ______________________________.

OFFICE COVERAGE AND PULPIT SUPPLY (If Needed)
(Estimated) ______________________________________.

TOTAL ESTIMATED RETREAT EXPENSES ______________.

Travel expenses. What form of transportation will be used? Calculate the cost of getting everyone to and from the retreat setting in a safe and dependable manner. Plan carefully so that you do not omit anyone who will need transportation to the retreat. When the group can travel together, it often adds to the anticipation of the event itself. Will you need ground transportation if you fly?

Accommodations. What is the cost for your team members to attend the retreat and have appropriate accommodations? In planning this kind of retreat, you probably will want your team members to have some privacy for reflection time. In this case, consider single occupancy rooms in your budget planning.

Meals. If you are going to a retreat setting, the cost of your accommodations may include your meals. If you are going to a standard motel setting, you will need to budget for the meals.

Team-Building Exercises. Since this is a professional development retreat, the reasonable cost of some recreation or entertainment should be included. Be sensitive to your church budget and the purpose of your retreat. Furthermore, you may plan a retreat for the team and their spouses at some time. While some recreational expenses may be better justified and benefited at a pastor-spouse retreat, it is vital to plan a casual, recreational activity as a part of your retreat if you intend to bring out the creative best of your team.

Retreat Leader/Facilitator. There is great value in having a guest come for part of your retreat to provide a challenge or listening ear to you and your team. Consultants from the Sunday School Board can be invited for local church events in some cases. You may invite a pastor from another church to come and provide a ministry to your team. State convention personnel may be willing and available in some cases. Nonetheless, you will want to provide the expenses for their travel, meals, accommodations, and an honorarium.

Materials. Accomplishing the desired results of the team retreat may require reading selected books, evaluating new resources, or renting special equipment to make the retreat meaningful. Estimate these expenses along with note pads, markers, tape, and any audio visual equipment needs that you anticipate.

Finally, plan for someone to preach, teach, or carry out the oversight of the church program in your congregation during the retreat. If you include your support team in the retreat, temporary support staff may be needed to answer the phones and provide the routines of managing the church office in your absence. One of the things you may want to do is invite the Director of Missions to use your office for the day. He can take care of any "pastoral emergencies" that may arise, while at the same time, probably would look forward to a day set aside on his calendar to use your office for a break in his routine. Having worked with several faithful and devoted denominational professionals, I know many would welcome a day to read in the setting of any one of our church offices.

A practical way to achieve the purposes identified in the team retreat may be to attend one of the conference centers such as Ridgecrest or Glorieta. During the summer, your team could take advantage of the training and excellent worship experiences planned by the Baptist Sunday School Board. There is something for everyone during weeks like the National Conference for Church Leadership. Reviewing the events of each day, or planning implementation meetings around scheduled conferences could effectively balance your achievement needs for a team retreat. The conference centers also are available during the "off season" for retreats with a variety of accommodations and price packages.

Once you have calculated the anticipated cost of this event, let your budget-planning team (or committee) review the expenses. Believing most churches want to provide the best tools and resources for our ministers, this planning should be honored. Giving attention to details in the first such retreat, and ensuring its success with improved and strengthened team performance should make subsequent planning easier.

Setting the Retreat Date

Once the budget is approved, set the date on the church calendar, and inform the members of your team of the retreat date. Some may need to make arrangements for child care or other personal issues. All will need to clear their calendar for this event if it is to be effective. The retreat is not optional. It is a required event except in the case of illness or death.

Give everyone time to plan for the retreat. Team members will need to make plans for their families. Childcare considerations, spouse work schedules, and individual ministry plans may require several months' notice in order for schedules to come together. In some cases, the church can assist by providing "surrogate grandparents" to the team members who have young children.

Your ability to be sensitive to the major calendar events of other pastors is always appreciated. The pastoral team is going to appreciate your sensitivity to their calendar. The week prior to the annual Easter pageant probably is not the best time to plan a retreat if you want the pastor who has responsibility for this event to be present, and both mentally and emotionally engaged.

Planning the Retreat Agenda

Next, plan the retreat. Over-planning will be better than under-planning. This is an expensive endeavor. Multiply the daily cost of maintaining the team to the church budget and you quickly see that the cost of the retreat is in reality more than what is budgeted for it. Do not waste the time of anyone participating.

Consider the best way of communicating your vision for the team. Use training films, computer assisted presentation media, audio-visual tools, and object lessons. Plan feedback and brain-storming sessions. Create an atmosphere for sharing by providing butcher paper, markers, tape, and round table seating.

Enlist each member of the team for specific responsibilities during the retreat. Have them give devotions or testimony pertinent to the retreat purpose. Give research assignments such as community surveys or layleader interview assignments to team members prior to the retreat. Interview members of your team using audio or video recordings, and play those recordings during the retreat at appropriate times.

If the retreat will include strategic calendar planning, have ample planning materials available such as blank calendar pads. It will be helpful to bring a calendar showing denominational events that will support some of your short- and long-range planning.

Numerous self-scoring inventories are available and will prove helpful for your pastoral team. These not only lend themselves to a retreat setting, but they also provide added insight for the ministry plans you may develop for the coming five years. Some of these inventories may have been used in your recruitment process, (discussed in Chapter 3) but if it has been over two years, it will be interesting to take them again to see how the team personality may have grown or matured.

The Retreat Pastor/Facilitator

If you are planning to have a guest challenge your team, enlist that individual the moment you have the budget approved and the date set. Remember that this is your retreat. If you enlist someone to challenge your team, define for them their allotted time. While a retreat pastor may seem unnecessary, there is a real advantage in having someone come and minister to the spiritual growth needs of pastoral-team members. Furthermore, if you are doing strategic planning, the insight and expertise of a mentoring, team-building pastor from another church, or even a gifted layman who specializes in planning, communicating, or motivating can be a valuable addition.

The guest needs to know your retreat purpose. Talk with this individual as you would a spiritual confidant. If there have been significant struggles in the church or even between members of the team, discuss this. Let this "retreat pastor" know some of the plans and dreams that are held by members of the team. Enlist someone who will be able to lead your team in worship. A retreat is a time for personal review and evaluation. Spiritual issues are always at the heart of what we do, especially goal setting and strategic planning. "Unless the Lord builds the house, They labor in vain who build it" (Ps. 127:1). Prayerfully enlist your "retreat pastor," or conclude that God wants you to lead this retreat.

The Retreat Before the Retreat

Plan each moment and begin the retreat by establishing an air of anticipation for it weeks before it actually takes place. Communicate with your team during team meetings your personal hopes for the retreat. If you have a theme, refer to it during the team devotionals in the weeks prior to the retreat. Write a personal card or letter to every member of your team in the days prior to the retreat to let them know that you are praying for them and looking forward to the time you will spend together. If you know a member of your team has been especially busy, require them to have a day off prior to the retreat, or at least a couple of nights at home during the week before. Knowing that the spouse is supportive and encouraging of the retreat will make it a better experience for everyone.

When the retreat date finally rolls around, plan on it being a significant time. Be positive and anticipate a good experience. A retreat can be an effective means of establishing or reevaluating the goals of the team. It is a time to review the team's work strategically. In some cases, priorities may be realigned. The ultimate goal is to retreat in order to go forward with greater strength and determination.

Benefits

Not only does a retreat give you an environment to establish new goals, it also is an environment that may enable you to improve relationships. In a retreat setting the typical interruptions that characterize the church office are left behind. You find yourself in an arena where people talk. Some even begin to listen in ways they have never done. The retreat setting can become holy ground! When relationships are strengthened, communication will no doubt improve too. There are some relationship building exercises that will assist you in creating this environment on your next retreat. *Adventure Rec,* a resource available from the Baptist Sunday School Board has several tips for planning retreats with activities designed to build trust and team spirit. *Adventure Rec* is listed in the appendix on the computer diskette with ordering information for your convenience.

Retreats also are great places to build team spirit. I am not certain that team spirit can be created. In fact, I'm almost certain that it cannot. The God who calls us into team relationships has to grace it upon us. When He does this, we need to enjoy it, cultivate it, protect it, anticipate it, and utilize it. When the team spirit grows cold, we have to find out how to rekindle its fire. In this way, team spirit can be built, strengthened, and even improved, but it seems presumptuous to say that we can create it.

A retreat setting gives the team-building pastor the opportunity to educating the rest of the team in new strategies for ministry. Planning a retreat to accomplish this purpose is a good idea in that it provides uninterrupted time for the team members to become exposed, familiar, and in some cases, committed to a new ministry strategy. While secular companies often review policy changes in retreat settings, these are best taken care of in weekly team meetings. The emphasis for a retreat involving this group of church leaders needs to be more inspirational that what is typically afforded in policy and procedure manuals.

Someone once said that your retreat will have marked success if you can do the following five things:

1. Identify a purpose and underscore it thematically.
2. Create an atmosphere that encourages sharing.
3. Balance planning and instruction with recognition and affirmation.
4. Help retreat participants avoid the "drowsies" by controlling the menu with “healthy foods.”
5. Conclude the retreat, or at least include in the retreat, a time of celebration.

Add to this a time for personal reflection or simply some appropriate blocks of free time, and you have the recipe for a retreat that will energize and renew the team for another 12 months. In the process of ministering effectively to the team, just think of the multiplied impact you have on ministering to an entire congregation. If the respective pastors return from the retreat “re-focused, re-freshed, and re-grouped,” they will minister out of the overflow to the congregation. In the end, everyone becomes revived!

CHAPTER 11

Rekindling the Team's Passions

The team builder is enabled by grace to remain focused in any situation. His biblical model is Jesus, who amidst the distractions "set his face to go to Jerusalem" (Luke 9:51). Another model could easily be Nehemiah, who refused to come down from the wall to negotiate with the antagonists who would only distract the passions implanted by the hand of God into the heart of the great rebuilder of broken walls. Paul is a model of the focused leader, saying "this one thing I do" (Phil. 3:13). Imprisoned, a survivor of every conceivable distraction that life could throw his way, yet he still focused on those things that God had before him.

Distractions come in many forms to the members of pastoral teams. Sometimes there are church antagonists who refuse to get their life right with God. At other times a building campaign can distract pastors from the main reason they are in ministry leadership positions. Pastoral counseling can devour the time-management skills of even the best team member. There are personal issues such as paying the mortgage, planing for the children's college education, poor health, troubled marriages, broken-down cars, and unresolved anger.

Whatever the form, the results can look strangely similar. Ministry output lessens, the joy begins to erode, the passion for ministry gets lost, and in the meantime, the grass begins to take on deeper shades of green in other places. Anyone in ministry (who is honest) will tell you that one of the greatest distractions to productive ministry is often the temptation to go to one of those other, greener places.

Shepherding the Team

What can a team builder do to help his team members remain focused? There are no easy answers, but here are some tips:

Be a shepherd, not a shamer. Shepherds are gentle with their flocks when distractions come. As a team leader, you have a responsibility to shepherd your team. You are their pastor as well as their vocational leader. Be sensitive to the spiritual battles that your team members may be facing. Lovingly seek entrée into their confidence and try to minister redemptively.

Provide career-assessment opportunities when a team member begins to show patterns of poor ministry performance or professional dissatisfaction. A potential change in a person's understanding of God's call may be behind the distraction. While this does not excuse ministerial incompetence, it may help explain why the passion for a particular area of ministry no longer exists. God's call does take on new challenges as we mature spiritually.

Exercise grace. The distraction may be deeper and much more personal than you initially detect. A team member who shows irritability at work may be having some very serious problems at home. When you exercise grace in addressing the improper attitude, you may discover the real problem and be better positioned to minister and restore the team.

Provide the resources needed for professional counseling. There are some emotional issues that require the help of trained professionals. Christian counselors may be able to assist a team member in times of trouble better than you can. This is not to be understood as a statement of your ability, but it recognizes the severity of the emotional issues that may be involved. Churches should provide adequate insurance for needs such as this, but when they don't, or even when they cover only partial expenses, a team member may be in need of assistance but too embarrassed to ask.

Be honest. Sometimes the distractions come as a result of problems in the church or rumors regarding the possibility of significant change. Deal with these possibilities openly and honestly.

Be willing to "care-front" your team member when the time is right. If you suspect a member of your team is involved in destructive behavior patterns rooted in sin, confront him or her about it and express concern for the persons's well being, physically and spiritually. Offer the same kind of help that you would offer anyone in your church. We rarely throw people away who stumble and fall. Even though we have "great expectations" of our team members, they are only human. Confront, express concern, offer support, and move to put the distraction in the past.

The Pastor-Staff Leadership Department of the Baptist Sunday School

Board provides resources for the many needs that are often discovered in any one of the above mentioned scenarios. Through LeaderCare, a preventative and restorative ministry, the Board is helping team members deal with life's distractions. If you or someone you know is having difficulties in any of these areas, please call us at 1-888-789-1911. The call is toll-free.

Personal Enrichment Expectations

In exploring the possibility that an individual might join your team, let them know of the personal enrichment expectations that you have of them. If you stand to inherit a team, discover the continuing education or personal enrichment opportunities that are offered before agreeing to move to the new ministry setting. This is important for several reasons.

First, you are interested in your own personal enrichment and growth. Leaders are lifelong learners. When we stop learning, we cease leading. You will want to set the pace for personal growth and development by modeling the benefits of conferences, seminars, refresher courses, and training events for the members of your team.

Second, you are interested in a growing and maturing team. Leaders do not want to manage, they want to lead, which implies that people are following. You can manage people in one spot. They never have to grow or develop in order to be managed. To be led, they have to move. The scenery is always changing for the leader. Followers need to see a change of scenery, too.

Third, you want the church to grow and mature. Everything mentioned about a growing team is true for a growing and maturing church. If the senior leader and the members of the team are excited about personal growth and enrichment, chances are others will catch on.

Finally, you know that the sharper your team becomes, the more they grow in Christian maturity and in the development of their ministerial skills, the more valuable they will become to the church and the greater the contribution they will make to the Kingdom. Team builders half-jokingly say that they want their team members to look good, because when the team looks good, the team leader looks good. While not necessarily a good motivation, it is more than "half true."

The Pastor Staff Leadership Department of the Baptist Sunday School is responding to this challenge through a lifelong learning process called LeaderSkill. LeaderSkill is designed to assist ministry professionals with the development of ministry skills in the areas of leading, communicating, administering, and ministering. Individual consultations and national training conferences are combined with cutting-edge resources to prepare God-called individuals for effective ministry into the twenty-first century.

The point of the previous paragraph is not to sound like a Board (bored) announcement. It is to say that there is no excuse for ministerial complacency. Expect the members of your team to grow and develop. Offer your team the best opportunity you can find for them to experience it. Inspect what they do and hold them to high accountability standards that will encourage them to share what they are learning and demonstrate what God is doing in their lives.

Spiritual Disciplines and How to Encourage Them

The most important area of growth is in the realm of *personal discipleship.* Not incidentally, the most virulent attack posing in the form of distractions will be aimed at the discouragement of the disciplines. If the life of Christ can be developmentally arrested in the life of your team members, Satan has won a battle. No amount of continuing education will make up for the failure to allow Christ to reproduce himself in and through us.

How then do team leaders encourage the disciplines?

There is no substitute for individual accountability. Some team leaders have put in the ministry covenants (job descriptions) of their team members the requirement for them to be involved in a small accountability group. Some team leaders even lead their teams in discipleship groups. This is a personal and very sensitive subject, but it affects team building in more significant ways than anything else in this book!

A team of growing disciples will lead a church of growing disciples. Discipleship is modeled. We model the life of Christ for others to see and literally catch. One of the values of the weekly team meeting is that it enables us to have a formal face-to-face discussion with the members of our team that is accountability intensive.

Bill Martin was not a member of my team. He was too valuable a layman for God ever to call him into vocational ministry. Bill called me often for lunch and when he did, I knew what to expect. His first question at the table was going to be "So, what is God showing you in your quiet time?" I loved that question, and I loved knowing Bill was going to ask it. It was one of the things that helped me remain faithful to my discipline of prayer and Bible reading.

The team builder has every right to ask a similar question of the members of his team. One way to ask the question in a less confrontational and subjective manner is to lead the team through a devotional commentary or a study such as *Experiencing God* or *The Mind of Christ.* There are some great resources available at your local Christian bookstore that might address a specific need you sense as team leader.

Beyond this, the team leader can and should encourage the development of the spiritual discipline of listening—specifically, *listening to God.* Encourage the members of your team to attend prayer retreats. Let team members have a day off for the purpose of meditation and contemplation. This cannot be done in most church office suites. Ask the members of your team to select a day, place it on your calendar, and help them prepare for a private prayer retreat by being sensitive to their schedule when the date rolls around.

Develop a reading list of devotional classics that have ministered to you and ask members of your team to read them so that you can talk about them at a team retreat.

The most effective way to encourage the development of spiritual disciplines is to model them consistently before your team. Share your heart with members of the team regarding the impressions God places on your heart. Don't be selective about the disciplines, either. There's something inconsistent about teaching people the value of fasting while traveling around the country in Learjets. Simplicity is a discipline, too! Do not brag about what you've sacrificed in the process of cultivating your disciplines, and do not make the exercise of your methods the object of adoration.

The absence of the disciplines is obvious. Flesh has control. Undisciplined people lie. They produce no fruit. They prefer darkness to light because their deeds are evil. If you have team members like this, "carefrontation" and confrontation are going to be unavoidable. People do not drift into the disciplines required for Christlikeness. And in this case, the danger is always in what they are drifting toward.

INTERACTIVE REFLECTION

If Satan were going to distract you or a member of your team today, what do you think he would use most effectively?

____

____

____

____

Is there a pattern of behavior that you need to address in one of your team members right now?

____

What is it?

____

____

____

If left to drift, what will probably happen?

____

____

____

What are you going to do about it?

____

____

____

CHAPTER 12

A Special Word for Pastor-Search Committees

Sunday morning is in full swing. The day is bright. Sunday School teachers report great attendance. The choir is robed and ready. The deacons are in place. You stand a little taller in the new suit you are wearing, shoes shinned, handkerchief impeccably folded to compliment the matching tie that is knotted intimidatingly under your chin. You enter to face a crowded sanctuary as the organ swells to full throttle. There is a sweet spirit in this place, and moments later, you notice that a pulpit committee is present as well.

Pulpit committees (or, as they have become known in the last two decades, "pastor-search committees") have a look all their own. Some are more discrete than others when listening to prospective candidates. They try to avoid recognition by using the "Noah Plan," sneaking into the church two by two. Others throw discretion to the wind by parking a 16-passenger van indiscriminately in the church parking lot, emerging with precision steps, KJV Bibles and little legal pads in hand. Like a panel of judges they sit together, filling an entire pew. It was long ago discovered that the average size of a pulpit committee need not exceed five members. Five adults can comfortably sit in a full-size automobile, travel a few hours from sun-up, and hear a prospective preacher with almost no one knowing any different. Of course, some of the parking-lot ushers are junior detectives. They have been known to call the sheriff to trace the license plates of any suspicious looking Buicks (the car of choice for most five-member pulpit committees) and find out within the hour what church in the corresponding county could be coming to call upon the preacher.

So this chapter is lovingly written to pastors and pastor-search committee members alike. Pastors need this because too often, sometimes when we least expect it, search committees come calling. Sometimes they don't. Search committees need this chapter because amid the superfluous opinions and strategies out there, no one seems to have a perfect approach for training this committee with an effective method, let alone the protocol that should be observed in making one of the most important decisions that a church will ever have to make.

Where and when do you get started?

Obviously, a church forms a search committee when a vacancy has been announced in the local church, or when (in the case of a new church) it is desired to find a pastor. In the case where the office of pastor becomes vacant there are many emotions, questions, and challenges to be faced by the congregation. If the senior pastor has resigned to accept the pastorate of another congregation, some may feel rejection. In some cases, there will be anger and disappointment. The reasons should be obvious, but they are rarely discussed.

The person who has occupied the position of pastor has been entrusted with confidences. People have come to him to discuss intimate details of their personal and spiritual lives. The pastor is the object of numerous affections. Children draw pictures of him in the pulpit. Ladies old enough to be his mother give him words of encouragement and at times, matronly words of correction. Men invite him to play golf, go fishing, or meet them for lunches with the business crowd. Preachers stand with their people during some of life's most significant transitions including weddings, births, baby dedications, baptisms, and deaths. For a pastor to leave, taking all those entrustments with him, is tantamount to a spouse leaving and filing for divorce. And this is when the transition is "good." Imagine what it is like when the pastor is "found out" or "thrown out."

The church business plan. Regardless of the "whys" that may result in the resignation of the senior pastor, every church needs to have a "business plan." In the church constitution and bylaws, a written provision should be found detailing what to do in the event of a pastoral resignation. If nothing exists, steps need to be taken to include this part of a church's business plan. A business plan is simply a plan detailing how a church will conduct business in the event of an emergency. It is frightening to know how many churches do not have a business plan. While it may not be common to your experience, emergencies happen all the time. Not only do pastors resign, they also die. Churches experience the loss of facilities due to fire. Litigation can bring the wheels of progress, along with operational cash flow, to a screeching halt. A business plan helps a congregation during difficult times such as these.

Steps to take in transition

One of the first concerns deals with the obvious question, "Who is going to fill the pulpit when we are without a senior pastor?" The business plan should call for the chairman of the deacons to assume a great deal of leadership. He will enlist pulpit guests as supply preachers until an interim can be selected. In addition to this the chairman of deacons normally appoints a pastor-search committee or requests a nomination procedure in keeping with the church's policy and history. In some churches, the nomination of an interim-pastor-search committee separate from the search committee is necessary. This committee has the immediate responsibility of finding for the congregation a suitable interim who will not only fill the pulpit each week, but also provide leadership to the congregation and be a pastoral care provider during the absence of a senior pastor.

The election or appointment of a pastor-search committee begins Phase One. During Phase One, *an interim pastor is secured.* The entire church spends many hours in prayer. This prayer time includes a time of prayerful listening. Members of the pastor-search committee may find great value in holding formal listening sessions with members of the congregation. These listening sessions will provide insight and guidance to the search committee as thy begin their task of finding a new pastor. The listening sessions may give the church an opportunity to experience a unique healing time following the resignation of a senior pastor. As people talk with the search committee, a renewed or refreshed commitment is often made to God, because the focus shifts from the pain of seeing a minister leave to the promise of knowing that God is in control and has a new pastor in mind for the congregation.

What to do first

The first thing that a search committee needs to do is lead the congregation to *develop a profile for the prospective new pastor.* This is not a presumptuous activity; it is a spiritual discipline! Without a profile, the committee will spend unnecessary hours and resources dealing with unqualified individuals desiring to be considered as pastoral candidates. The profile begins with the scriptural qualifications for leaders found in 1 and 2 Timothy, and 1 Peter 5.

Such things as a commitment to missions and missions support should be considered. The profile may include the candidate's educational background, his ministry experience, his family life, and his philosophy of ministry. An excellent resource to study is *Kingdom Leadership: A Call to Christ-Centered Leadership* by Dr. Michael D. Miller.

Educational and academic preparations for ministry are no guarantee that spiritual strength and vitality will follow. However, in a day when professional competency is demanded in every area of life, it seems crucial to consider an individual's commitment to professional and intellectual development. The profile should indicate the minimal degree required for consideration. Seminaries offer a variety of degrees to prepare people for church leadership positions other than that of senior pastor. Religious education degrees or music degrees prepare those who are called to religious education or music ministry positions. However, these degrees do not include the academic tools needed for the task of pastoring today's church, nor do they offer the same mentoring and shaping value that will be a part of a Master of Divinity (MDiv) degree. If God calls a man late in life to change directions in his ministry, then God is probably calling that man to retrain and prepare for the new ministry, too. Furthermore, committees need to be careful when evaluating the academic preparations a man claims to have. An honorary or mail-order degree is not equivalent to an earned degree such as a Doctor of Theology (Th.D.), Doctor of Philosophy (Ph.D.), or Doctor of Ministry (D.MIN.) degree. Men who have taken shortcuts to the title "doctor" will probably take shortcuts in their work in the local church as well. It makes you wonder about their motivation in obtaining a title.

Similarly, committees should exercise caution in reviewing the "ministerial experience" of candidates. There is a difference between a man who has had ten years of pastoral experience and a man who has had two years of experience five times. Long tenure tells a committee much about the candidate's ability to serve long-term and to get along with people. Certainly God calls individuals to short pastoral tenures. However, one of the factors involved in the growth of the church is long pastoral tenure. Churches usually are not looking for a new pastor who will only stick around a couple of years. They are hoping to find "a keeper."

The committee may want to consider prayerfully the size of the active membership of the church in the prospective candidate's present location. For example, a church that runs 650 in worship that is presently pastorless has already been led to overcome the unique growth barriers of churches much smaller. If a person is pastoring a church with a much smaller active membership, they may not have all of the skill competencies necessary to lead a 650 member church to continued growth. The new pastor should have experience in leading the congregation to pass the next series of unique growth barriers. This may not always be true! Remember, God looks on the heart while we can only look on the surface. If His leading is clear, never hesitate. Yet, you may find His leading in the establishment of a profile, and His undeniable blessing in staying with it!

A Sample Profile

Let's imagine a pastoral profile for XYZ Baptist Church. This church has an average of 500 in Sunday School and 650 in worship. XYZ is a church with a strong history of starting new missions and giving to mission projects within the denominational structure. The former pastor left to begin teaching in a seminary. The church is in a growing neighborhood with strong possibilities for the future.

PASTORAL PROFILE

Salvation Experience:

The candidate needs to have experienced at least 15 years of consistent Christian growth since conversion.

Call to Ministry:

The candidate must be able to articulate clearly a call to preach, and this must be clearly recognized by others who know the candidate.

Educational Background:

The candidate must have the basic seminary degree recommended for senior pastors, including concentrations in theology, pastoral work/preaching, and church administration (Master's of Divinity). An earned doctorate is not required but is preferred.

Ministerial Experience:

- The candidate needs to have experience in leading a church with a membership range of 600–1000 members and experience leading a pastoral team of other ministry professionals.
- He needs to have building experience since this church is in need of new buildings for continued growth.
- The candidate will have at least one church experience where he served for five years.
- The candidate needs to be a personal soul winner with a strong baptismal ratio in the church of at least 20:1 or to be able to point to a 5–10 % growth ratio in baptisms for the past two years.
- The candidate needs to have strong interpersonal relationship skills, strong work habits, and denominational loyalty.

Gifts and Passions:

- The candidate must possess strong pulpit skills.
- The candidate must have a strong and growing prayer life.
- The candidate must have a pastor's heart demonstrated by the care shown in his present church.

Because this church will not discriminate on the basis of age or race, we invite all nominations from members of the congregation in keeping with the above profile.

Once the profile has been developed and accepted by the congregation, the committee is ready to begin receiving resumés. Under no circumstances should the committee receive any resumé from anyone until the profile has been completely developed and accepted by the congregation. There will be many in the congregation who would like to recommend someone they know to the position of pastor. Some will be more qualified than others. The profile gives the committee a minimum standard from which to work. It frees them to take the prayerful support of the congregation, the information gathered in listening sessions, and the unique insight given them by the Holy Spirit and concentrate responsibly on the task before them.

At this point, the committee should begin to review resumés. A set date should be announced to the church for the reception of resumés. After this date, the committee should begin a prayerful review of every resumé received. Following an agreed upon time of prayer, committee members should meet to narrow the field of candidates by eliminating resumés that fall outside the parameters of the profile.

Following this, the committee moves into a more prayerful review. Committee members should be asked to pray specifically for insight into the needs of the church. When the committee reconvenes, members should be asked to share their impressions regarding concerns about the congregation as a whole and concerns about the needs of individuals in the church. Committee members should recall the vision for the church's future ministry. Including other members of the pastoral team in this meeting may be wise. They have insight that can be a benefit to the committee. A committee can offer great affirmation to the members of the pastoral team during this time, but they should never let the members of the pastoral team impact the direction or the decisions being made as a committee. The one exception is to hear negative reference material about a candidate that the committee may never hear in any other way.

A series of questions needs to be answered by the Search Committee during this time to prepare them for questions that will no doubt be raised in the future. These questions may include:

- What is the purpose statement of this church?
- Where do we see ourselves in five years?
- What will a new pastor find as he moves to this field of service?
- What are the strengths of this church?
- What are the reasons a pastor would want to come to this church?

Once the members of the committee understand the positive aspects for a prospective pastor, they should seek to take an honest look at the possible negatives. Committee members should listen prayerfully to one another as well as to the pastoral staff during this time. When the committee members know the challenges, demands, and potential difficulties facing a prospective pastor, they will be better prepared to review the resumés covering a man's training and experience that would uniquely qualify him for this ministry.

Following this series of meetings, set a time for the next meeting, giving members at least two weeks to prayerfully consider all of the remaining resumés. Their assignment is to return to the next meeting with a "short list" of five candidates. It is not uncommon for this part of the process to require more than one meeting. The chairman of the search committee should be encouraging and sensitive to every member of the committee. If someone is having a difficult time with schedules, there may be a need to move a committee alternate to active status, replacing this individual. This should only be done as a last resort and only after several delays or schedule problems. The process of finding a new pastoral candidate is time consuming. Remember this, and proceed only as the Lord clearly indicates.

The short list of five names should only be compared at this meeting, and it should not be publicized. Do not fall guilty to the accusation that you are staging a "beauty contest" by comparing multiple candidates. The reason you are moving to a list of five names is so that you can determine the direction God is giving to the committee. If the variety of lists are incomparable, you know that more time is needed for consideration. More potential candidates may be needed. Do not panic. God is sovereignly in control of the entire process, and His timing is perfect.

It may become necessary to allow committee members to discuss their convictions before arriving at a consensus regarding the short list. Someone may see a quality or characteristic that no one else noticed. Meeting to discuss committee members' lists can help refine and refresh the committee's perspective. The goal is to move to a list of names that, by consensus, the committee feels meets the profile. These are now referred to as "potential candidates." Once this is done, the committee is ready for Phase Two of the search process.

Phase Two is to visit the church of each potential candidate for the purpose of evaluating preaching and worship leadership skills. In recent years, search committees have begun requesting video tapes of potential candidates. While this seems economical, it is a poor substitute for visiting in person. There are many things that will never be captured on video tape. Also, nonprofessional recordings can give a committee a less-than-accurate impression of a candidate.

This preliminary visit need not be announced. You are still in the information-gathering stages. Do not schedule interviews yet. During these visits, plan to listen, observe, and participate in worship. Listening to these men preach and lead their church in worship will give you more insight into their abilities and gifts than any interview will.

Following each individual visit, the committee should meet to discuss their observations. Evaluating this experience should take time. In addition to the obvious interest that you will have in the sermon's content and the preacher's delivery, you will want to observe many other things. Answer the following questions:

- What seemed to be the dynamic between the pastor and the other worship leaders?
- What did you observe about the interpersonal skills of each pastor with his people?
- How were you welcomed in this church?
- Did anyone speak to you?
- Did they say anything about their pastor to you?
- What did the worship guide say to you about the priority of this church?
- What were the strengths and weaknesses of the church as you saw it during this visit?
- Did anything offend you in this worship experience?
- Would you want to attend this church again if you were a newcomer to the community?
- Would you consider joining this church?

It may seem an expensive or extravagant use of church funds to travel so much. In reality, this will be a valuable investment in the congregation's livelihood. If shortcuts seem necessary to the committee or to the church, the church really is not ready to take the step of calling and supporting a new pastor. There are less expensive ways to search, but the end product is not always as satisfying as this more detailed approach.

After the committee has visited each pastor on the short list, *a prioritized list should be made.* The committee should not move forward until this list becomes ordered from one to five with all in agreement on the order of candidates to be considered. Once this happens, the committee is ready to engage candidates in dialogue regarding the possibility of their becoming the church's next pastor. If after the visits the committee feels the candidates are no longer potential, begin the process over. Share the steps taken by the committee with the congregation (leaving out the names considered) and request the church's prayers for direction.

If one or more potential candidate visits resulted in good worship experiences for the committee members, you may be ready to prioritize the candidates. If not, visit the candidates in their churches at random again in the same way that you did earlier. When prioritization is accomplished, you are prepared to enter Phase Three of the search.

Phase Three should include a phone call to the number one candidate by the committee chairman. Introducing himself, the chairman should tell the pastor of the committee's recent visit and their impressions. Let him know that your committee would like to know if he is open to an exploratory interview regarding your church's vacancy. If so, plan a date for a second visit so that the committee can return to the church to hear him preach and lead in worship and can meet with him following the morning worship service. Volunteer to answer any questions the pastor may have and be prepared to provide printed information about the church and the community for him.

On the date of the scheduled *exploratory visit,* continue to be as discreet as possible. Communicate all of the lunch arrangements with the candidate prior to the Sunday morning visit. If he has younger children, offer to provide a sitter, or at least be willing to pay for one of his choosing so that he and his wife will be able to engage more aggressively with members of the committee.

Let the pastor recommend a meeting place for lunch. Motels often provide meeting rooms and will cater a lunch providing more privacy than most local restaurants. The chairman may suggest this as an alternative and then take the initiative to make the arrangements. A restaurant would be a nice place to meet, but be aware that on Sundays the candidate will feel awkward if he thinks other members of his church might see him eating with a table full of strangers. It becomes obvious quickly to even the novice Christian that scouts are attempting to lure his pastor away. Ask him for suggestions on a restaurant or other meeting place (across town, at a hotel, in a nearby city, etc.), and then make all the arrangements for a productive meeting.

Know that the interview is 50-50. Half of it belongs to the candidate, half of it belongs to the committee. Ask questions and expect to be asked questions. Both parties involved need to probe and discover as much about each other as possible. The committee members need to be up-front regarding salary administration, benefits, expectations, responsibilities, and opportunities. Have a fact folder prepared showing the salary range, the benefit schedule, continuing education commitments, vacation time, annuity/retirement, professional expenses that will be provided, and resources that are available including support team personnel. Include a synopsis of the church history and vision statements. Gather growth statistics and baptismal records for the previous three years. Include an area map and information regarding schools, the economy, a realtor's brochure showing available housing, and a recent newspaper.

Following this exploratory visit, both parties need time to reflect and pray. Set up a time for a future phone call between chairman and candidate, and dismiss early enough so that the minister's family can rest and resume their normal Sunday schedule as much as possible.

The committee needs to convene immediately to discuss the exploratory interview. It should be easy to be positive at this point, but the committee needs to be honest to the point of criticism. You are considering a man who will have many decisions to make. You represent an entire congregation. Much has gone into the process. Do not grow weary and proceed with the motivation just to be finished. Once you call a new pastor, it is only the beginning!

If the committee is still enthusiastic, the chairman needs to call the candidate on the agreed-upon date to find out if an informal interview is desirable. An *informal interview* is more serious than an exploratory one, but it is not formal to the point of extending a call. The informal interview should take place in the community of the committee's church. This way, the candidate can see the community, the church campus and facilities, get a feel for the ministry challenges, and further discern God's hand in the process. The spouse should be invited for the same reasons, but she should not feel obligated to participate in the interview.

The church will want to provide travel expenses and all accommodations for the candidate during this visit. The informal interview should consist of follow-up questions from the exploratory interview, along with questions relative to pastoral care, theology, and ministry philosophy. The candidate should be encouraged to clarify anything regarding the salary structure, church finances, church administration, and expectations. If copies of the church's constitution and by-laws have not already been given to the candidate, they should be presented to him in this meeting. (It is preferable to give this printed matter along with the fact folder prior to the exploratory meeting.)

Again, a time should be determined to follow up this meeting, giving both parties the time to pray and seek the Lord's will. The search committee should prayerfully evaluate the candidate's answers to questions raised during this informal interview. They should critically address any unresolved differences that surfaced. If the committee is unanimous, they should recommend to the chairman that a formal interview be scheduled.

The formal interview normally encompasses an entire weekend. During the formal interview, the prospective pastor brings his entire immediate family with him and is given the opportunity to meet with several leadership groups within the church. A deacons-wives banquet or a Sunday School leadership banquet is a great way of bringing together as many church leaders as possible, giving the candidate the opportunity to be introduced and providing the first opportunity for him to be heard by members of the church. A Friday- or Saturday-night banquet generally works well. Sometime during the formal weekend, the pastoral team needs to have the opportunity to meet the candidate. This meeting could last several hours and should be facilitated briefly by the chairman of the search committee. Following introductions and a brief question-and-answer time, the candidate and the existing team should be given some time alone. At some time the search committee needs to have a final interview during which no single question is left unasked and no detail is left unresolved or in need of further clarification.

It may be difficult for the candidate to observe a worship service in this interview time due to responsibilities that are still priorities in the candidate's present church. If this is so, attempt to structure the banquet setting so that it reflects the spiritual passion of the congregation. The formal interview ends, and the search committee needs to do one final, deliberative evaluation. In view of everything that has been said and exchanged, the committee must decide if this is the man God wants to serve as the next pastor of the church. If so, share this decision with the groups involved in the formal interview weekend. Unless there is a strong opposition from those invited to meet with the candidate, you are ready to enter Phase Four.

Phase Four is when you ask the candidate if he is willing to come and preach to the entire congregation in view of becoming the next pastor of the

church. The candidate may need some time to pray about it. Arrive at a reasonable time for this prayer to be answered. Generally, no more than one week should be needed. The process has been a prayerful one. The three interviews have progressed with intensity and purpose. If the candidate needs more than one week to decide if God is in this or not, you have to decide what is reasonable and what is not. Be firm, but do not be pushy.

Provided the candidate is willing, outline a time-table. First, determine when he and his family are available to come to your church to preach in the morning and evening services. Determine when your church will cast a vote to "call" this man as your pastor. Determine or communicate what is required by your constitution to extend a call. Determine an acceptance date by which time the candidate will either accept or reject the call. Stick to this date. Know when the transition date will take place, and be prepared to share this with the congregation when the vote is taken. Communicate these dates in writing with the candidate and with the committee.

When the Big Day Finally Arrives

Err on the side of graciousness and generosity. Do everything possible to make this a significant day in the life of the candidate and your church. You have worked hard for months to get to this point. By giving attention to detail, you will protect against a last-minute disaster. The chairman of the search committee should introduce the candidate to the congregation with little detail regarding the search process. That should be communicated in church mail the week prior to the "Call Sunday." The worship service should be planned so that the candidate can lead in worship as he would normally do on Sunday. A testimony time would be appropriate in the morning service along with the sermon.

Following the evening message, a vote should be taken by the church. The results of this vote should be completely communicated with the candidate. When he communicates his decision with the chairman of the search committee, it should be shared with the congregation immediately. Normally, this takes place the night the vote is taken or prior to the following Sunday morning.

Transitional issues and getting started are wonderful subjects for another book. See the appendix located on the computer disk for a checklist regarding salary administration issues for pastoral team members. Moving expenses (some of which are taxable at the writing of this book) are covered in this resource.

Some Closing Thoughts

Do's for Pastor-Search Committees

- Keep all prospective candidates informed of your committee's progress in writing. Every résumé received should be acknowledged as a courtesy. A form letter is sufficient for this purpose.
- Let potential candidates know that they have been excluded from the search process by returning their résumés and any additional information such as tapes, videos, and photographs. Thank them for their interest and simply inform them that God has given other direction at this time.
- When you arrive at a short list of potential candidates, inform those on the list of your progress and your status in the process. You do not need to tell them their rank on the short list. In fact, it is inadvisable to do so. Let them know of your continued prayers. In some cases, since this is a prayer process, you may receive a letter from someone on the short list requesting that they no longer be considered as a candidate. God answers our prayers in many different ways.
- Know that the candidates may feel a hesitation to call you for updates on the committee's progress. Their hesitation to call should not be interpreted as non-interest. Stay in touch as a courtesy. It is sometimes much easier for potential candidates to talk when you call them at home in the evenings rather than at the church office. Be considerate of their desire for confidentiality.
- Before you begin corresponding with listed references provided by a candidate, let him know of your intention. In some cases, a reference may be a member of the candidate's church or his pastoral team. Give him the opportunity to share the process before you begin contacting these individuals.
- Be prompt with any reimbursable expenses the candidate may incur in travel to informal and formal interviews.
- Be sensitive to family schedules and concerns of the candidate.
- Exercise discretion and protect the confidentiality of the process at all times.

Some Don'ts for the Search Committee

- Don't rush the process.
- Don't discuss the progress or share information regarding the potential candidates with anyone other than the members of the committee.
- Don't expect to find a pastor who is just like the one who recently left your church.
- Don't mislead the candidate when it comes to answering the difficult questions.
- Don't move forward without conviction.

Some Do's for the Potential Pastoral Candidate

- Remember that all interviews are 50-50. You should ask as many questions as a prospective committee. There are no "off-limits" questions.
- Be gracious. It is an honor to be considered by a search committee as a potential candidate.
- Remain focused. There is little that will ever compare in its capacity to distract a pastor from his responsibilities like being contacted by a search committee. God has you in a strategic place for a definite purpose. Remain faithful to that until it is clear that He has released you.
- Provide information that is requested by the committee within reason.

Some Don'ts for the Potential Pastoral Candidate

- Don't announce to your congregation that you are "being considered" too early in the process. This only serves effectively to remove any leadership potential that you have in your present church. If things do not work out for any reason, you appear wounded and thrown back, rejected and humiliated to your present congregation who may have been very excited at the prospects of your soon departure.
- Don't announce your resignation too soon. If you have received a call from a congregation, announce your acceptance quickly and resign from your present church. You will find that preaching only two additional sermons prior to your departure will seem like an eternity. Resign giving a two weeks notice unless your constitution requires more time.
- Don't be critical of your church in the final days of your ministry there. If things have been difficult, see God's call as a deliverance. Celebrate

the deliverance in your personal worship, but do not stoop to negative talk regarding the church. Leave in such a way that the church would be glad to see you return should God ever call you back.

- Don't attempt to give too much guidance to the church as you prepare to leave. Train your chairman of deacons, give instruction to your pastoral team, but see God's calling to a new church as God's calling away from the present church.
- Don't be surprised at the reactions you get from church members and team members when you announce your intentions to leave. There will be anger, shock, resentment, fear, distrust, and, at times, grief. Some will be happy for you and your family as you face new opportunities and challenges. Others will be disappointed, never accepting the possibility that God was in the process.

One More Thing Before You Go

As difficult as it may seem in some cases, one of the greatest things that could be done when a ministry comes to a close for a pastor is to *conduct an exit interview.* Corporate America does this in order to become stronger. It is one of the "CEO" feeling things that might be very valuable for the church and the exiting pastor. An exit interview will provide several benefits.

Church leaders will have an opportunity to ask any "hard questions" of the exiting pastor such as "What could we have done that would have made your ministry here more meaningful?" and "What are the positive things that you would tell a prospective pastor about our church, and what are the negative things?"

The pastor should have the same opportunity to ask questions like this so that he can better understand the "dis-ease" that may have prompted him to view his leaving as the call of God.

There are other valuable benefits to the exit interview. It gives everyone involved the opportunity to bring closure in some practical matters such as returning church property and keys to the building, confirming unused vacation time, and making sure that all reimbursable expenses are balanced on both ends.

INTERACTIVE REFLECTION

This chapter is written for both the pastor and the pastor-search committee. What did you find most helpful in this chapter that will be of use to you in the years ahead?

____

____

____

____

____

If you are a team builder or mentor to other pastors, what do you think they need to keep in mind when considering God's call to a new church? What do they need to ask a prospective search committee when first contacted?

____

____

____

____

____

If you serve on a search committee, do you have the following?

- o Your church purpose statement
- o A profile for your next prospective pastor
- o A commitment to finding the best man possible regardless of how far you might have to go to find him

CHAPTER 13

Dealing with Accusations Against a Team Member

It generally begins with a phone call to the pastor-leader by a member of the body requesting an appointment. What ensues causes concern to the team leader. Knotting the stomach and intensifying the stress-related headache characteristic of leadership, you listen as a church member begins to unfold a six--month diatribe detailing the inadequacies, incompetencies, and in some cases, the immoral behavior of a member of your team.

If it has not happened to you, chances are it will. It is the nature of our day. Accusations against a member of your team, particularly those brought to your attention by members of the body, are serious business. Being the leader of the team and being the spiritual leader of the congregant sitting in your office require administrative accuracy and skillful precision if you are going to continue being the leader in either sphere with any credibility. What you do in times such as this defines the depth of your leadership ability as a team builder.

I write this chapter with incredible sensitivity to spiritual warfare. "Your adversary the devil, as a roaring lion, walketh about, seeking whom he may devour," wrote Peter in a word of caution to pastors (1 Pet. 5:8). When seeking to destroy the credibility of a church or an individual minister, there is rarely anything as effective as a leveled accusation. Regardless of the facts involved, the accusation alone becomes incriminator, jury, and judge, immediately rendering a life sentence of suspicion and presumed guilt. Regardless of facts, accusations carry the power to destroy credibility, unity, and ministry effectiveness.

Knowing how to deal with accusations no longer is an optional topic at a conference center; it is a mandatory discipline for the leaders of today's churches. Perspective is important. In this instance, God's perspective is priceless.

Against an elder receive not an accusation, but before two or three witnesses. (1 Tim.5:19)

God's Word sets forth a primary principle every team builder needs to know. In many cases, this word alone is enough to silence the issue and calls for no further investment on your part other than prayerfully to warn a member of your team in private that an individual came to you with an accusation. You will encounter spiritual opposition on many occasions as a leader of God's people. Nehemiah's resistance to come off the wall is our model when it comes to petty distractions. What Paul tells Timothy should be the model for the team builder whenever someone comes to make an accusation against one of your team members. Once the agenda is known, interrupt and show them that Scripture requires one other witness.

Levels of Accusation

For the sake of clarity, let's identify three levels of accusation. Level one accusations are in reality complaints, not accusations. They are minor but time-consuming issues. Level two accusations most often deal with skill performance or personality differences between members of the team and respected or at least active (these are not always one and the same) members of the congregation. Level three accusations are based upon moral or ethical issues and sometimes are the most difficult to discern. Level three accusations are potentially the most destructive accusations to the life of the body and the credibility of the team.

Level one accusations. Level one accusations deal with misunderstandings and are trivial to everyone involved except, of course, the accuser. Generally, level one complaints or accusations are the result of unresolved negative impressions innocently made by the pastor in question to the individual accuser.

Most level one accusations are best handled by using the biblical model of reconciliation. Team-leader involvement is not required but often is effective. By telling the accuser that they need to go to the offending pastor for a face-to-face confrontation, you follow a biblical principle. You can encourage this by picking up the intercom and asking the team member to join you in your office to answer their accuser. Chances are, you will no longer have to deal with level one accusations from this individual again.

If the accusation is made in earnest, the level one accuser may seem embarrassed but will be thankful for the opportunity to reconcile the misunderstanding. Knowing that you will point them toward biblical reconciliation, they will appreciate your leadership and respect you for the guidance you've given.

Level one accusations are single-incident issues that do not entail moral failures. Hurt feelings may be involved, but there has been no criminal nor malicious act. They can involve overlooking an appointment, chewing gum while leading in worship, failing to return a phone call, or not speaking to a person in a way that would make him or her feel important.

These accusations are important to the one bringing them. The team builder must rely on spiritual discernment in order to see the real motive behind the accusation. In dealing with level one accusations a sincere but quick and direct response that puts the burden of responsibility back on the accuser is proper and in reality an opportunity for grace. Memorize verses of Scripture such as Romans 12:18, "If it be possible, as much as lieth in you, live peaceably with all men," and Matthew 6:12, 14–15, "And forgive us our debts, as we forgive our debtors. . . . For if ye forgive men their trespasses, your heavenly Father will also forgive you: But if ye forgive not men their trespasses, neither will your Father forgive your trespasses." Level one accusations can become tedious and time consuming if encouraged. Be firm with your responses and deny any ownership or responsibility beyond directive involvement. In other words, do not trivialize your ministry office by becoming a conflict mediator for level one accusations. It is enough that you listen, apply the Word of God, and give the accuser something to do.

One final word regarding level one accusations: They often come to the team builder's attention through the mail. The best and most gracious way to handle this type of accusation is to write a personal note on the stationary upon which the original letter is written, and return it in the mail to the sender. Your personal note may in effect say, "Thank you for sharing this concern with me. I'll be praying for you as you seek the biblical response to broken fellowship with this person." Reference Romans 12:18 and Matthew 6:12–15, initial it, and return it in the mail that same day.

Do not waste an entire morning attempting to respond to the letter of a level one accuser by carefully writing a detailed defense designed to soften and even clear up the accusation. You have better things to do with your time. Any letter you might write requires your investment, and you do not own this issue. Don't enter the market!

Level two accusations. Level two accusations are much more serious. They can deal with perceptions that have been observed over a period of time. They are "broken camel's back" issues. Their content includes competency complaints communicated by comments such as: "We are not being fed." "Our children are never included." "Our authority is being undermined by everything that is being taught." "He's never prepared." "She is invariably unprofessional." "He consistently makes up excuses." Making matters worse, level two accusations can come from reliable sources and the people you respect. When you point them toward steps for biblical confrontation, they quickly tell you, "Been there; done that."

Sitting in front of you are two witnesses. Though they may be married, they still constitute what is necessary for you to take a few corrective measures. Remember, with level two accusations, you normally have a deeper level of respect and trust for the character of the accuser. They may be seeking a redemptive response, or they may be past that point. Nonetheless, at this moment you are the leader. You must show yourself as a leader and move this to your priority list. In most cases, the people in our church may forgive us for making a decision with which they disagree. They will not forgive us if we fail to make a decision. Leaders know this. Here are some important steps to take.

Intake: The team builder is going to listen to the accusation first for the purpose of *intake.* All of the pertinent facts need to be recorded for the purpose of assessing the situation. Ask the accusers for documentation of any event and share with them a copy of an "Incident Documentation Form" (see sample or use the form provided on the 3.5 computer disk entitled Incident.txt).

As a part of the intake session, the team builder needs to ask the persons making the accusation for permission to share the accusation with the team member in question. If the accusers say no to this request, the team builder has to put the responsibility back in the lap of the accusers. Never own their accusation, and never be owned by it.

If permission is granted, the team builder needs to take a copy of the notes from the intake session along with copies of the Incident Documentation Form, and schedule a meeting with the team member in question. It is a considerate procedure to provide the Incident Documentation Form to the accused team member prior to your scheduled meeting. Hitting them "out of the blue" with reports of an accusation will only serve to make them defensive and create an atmosphere devoid of trust between the two of you. More importantly, by giving them a copy of the documented accusation, you can ask the accused team member to prepare an Incident Documentation Form detailing their view of the situation. The Incident Documentation Forms are intended to be one-page summation forms, not running commentaries. Giving your team member one to two hours to review the Incident Documentation Form submitted by their accuser and to prepare one themselves is sufficient time. Prior to your scheduled meeting, obtain a copy of your team member's Incident Documentation Form and read it.

Interview: Set the tone for the team member interview by being as honest as you can, yet as calm as possible. Pray together, recognizing the element of spiritual warfare that is involved. Affirm your team member and relay your appreciation for their willingness to meet to discuss the documented incident.

Ask the team member if they would like to say anything before you begin discussing the incident. Be a listener and a friend during this time, regardless of what has been written by either party. Stay with the incident before you.

The Incident Documentation Form may point out several inconsistencies. If so, it is possible to discern further the magnitude of the accusation. It may be a misunderstanding. It could be something that was done, or innocently not done. If so, steps to reconciliation may be just around the corner.

In other circumstances the Incident Documentation Form may underscore the truth and the validity of the accusation. In cases like this, correction and instruction must be a part of the reconciliation or resolution phase.

This can be a growing time for an emotionally or spiritually immature team member. They may look back on this incident years later and be thankful that someone cared enough to confront. When incidents are valid and are met by team members in an honest spirit of repentance, reconciliation is possible, ministry effectiveness can continue, and the team can actually be strengthened.

In other situations, disciplinary actions may be required. In level two accusations, the offense has been observed over a period of time. It is not a one-time occurrence of ministerial incompetence; it is a pattern. It may even be possible for a probationary period to be established for the offending team member. During this time, supervision must be intensified and follow-up sessions must take place with the accusers involved in the incident documentation.

Investigation: Unfortunately, the disparity between Incident Documentation Forms may be so great that further investigation is required. This will require sensitivity to the people involved, proper assessment of all motives represented, and knowledge of the situation. Without passing the buck, *the dependence upon personnel-committee or administrative-ministry-team leadership will become valuable at this time.* Additional resources may include other lay leaders who may have knowledge of the situations detailed in the incident documentation. They can provide insightful history if needed.

Instruction. Regardless of the results of the investigation, when level two accusations go this far, instructions are going to be the minimal expectation for the team member. The instructions may include directions to improve skills and competencies. They may include steps for reconciliation. Often, effective instructions can be given to avoid the appearance of evil and, if necessary, to avoid any future contact with the accuser.

The issue of a level two accusation is never over without a follow-up meeting between the pastor and the accusers. Do not expect this to be a time of celebration. More often than not it only serves to inform the accusers that you have taken the matter seriously and have begun steps to see that it does not happen again. For those willing to exercise grace, this will be sufficient. For others, especially those with unresolved conflict patterns and non-surrendered power and control needs, nothing short of terminating the team member will satisfy. That you are not willing to offer such a sacrifice becomes a new area of contention and the conflict only broadens. We will address this more fully in the following pages dealing with antagonism.

The greatest possible scenario is to experience complete reconciliation between all parties during these times. The accusers are motivated by Jesus' words in Luke 17:3. "Take heed to yourselves: If thy brother trespass against thee, rebuke him; and if he repent, forgive him."

Team members are similarly motivated by God's Word. Even if everything was a complete misunderstanding with no intention to cause harm, the valuable team member does not want anything to come into his life that would cause him to become incapable of really worshiping God. Jesus sets the standard in Matthew's Gospel by saying, "Therefore if thou bring thy gift to the altar, and there rememberest that thy brother hath ought against thee; leave there thy gift before the altar, and go thy way; first be reconciled to thy brother, and then come and offer thy gift" (Matt. 5:23–24). Spiritually maturing team members know that the enemy may use anything in their lives to cause offense to others. They will aggressively seek reconciliation so that the cause of Christ will not suffer in them personally or corporately.

Level three accusations. Satan cannot stand to see the church of Jesus Christ prosper. When churches experience healthy growth, when thy are used mightily of God to change communities, when they aggressively pursue the gates of hell and the strongholds of Satan, he reacts with vengeance. The church sees this in many different manifestations. One of the most effective is to ruin a ministry with a level three accusation against a minister.

Level three accusations are potential headline makers. They include moral failures and unethical behaviors. While level three accusations can be limited to a minor "breach of church covenant" or an unresolved level two accusation that has ignored the prescriptive instructions given and failed at genuine reconciliatory efforts, they are generally more severe.

Making things more difficult, level three accusations can come from people who are known and respected, and they can come from complete strangers. The team builder cannot afford to mishandle anything related to a level three accusation. The credibility of the entire ministry of the church is on the line, not to mention the ministry futures of those involved in the accusation.

First, stay calm. You need to be able to see the accusation clearly and remember that unless you have firsthand knowledge of wrong doing, your team member may in fact be innocent.

The second thing you need to do is gather all of the information that is available. Listen to the charge being made very carefully. Listen for details such as dates, times, places, persons involved, and witnesses who can corroborate or clarify the accusation. If a criminal offense is implied in the accusation, express appropriate concern for the individuals harmed, but do not say anything that could further implicate the individual team member, other members of the team, or the church. Again, stay calm and listen.

It is going to be necessary to make either a confirmation or a confrontation in a level three issue at some point. Depending on the circumstances of the accusation, that time may be immediate, as in calling the team member in to face the accusation on the spot. A better plan is to evaluate quickly the extent of damage that could already be done if the accusation is true and make the confrontation controlled and formal. If the issue involves a moral or ethical question, it is possible that the team member has planned for a confrontation of sorts and is prepared in some way to bring further disgrace or harm to his accusers, his church, or even his team leader, who represents his church.

You are dealing with an emotionally charged, sensitive issue in level three accusations. For the welfare of everyone involved, remember that it is probably wise to keep the accuser and the accused in separate settings until you know more fully what you are facing. While your team member may be innocent, the accuser may believe in their heart that guilt is evident and even attempt to take justice into their own hands.

A formal confrontation will certainly involve others whose mere presence indicates prayer support and personal concern for the team member. It is vital that in this confrontation time someone is present to represent the appropriate authorities that have been violated, layleaders from the congregation, and in some cases the local law enforcement.

The team builder has been one credited with the ability to recognize where his spiritual gifts and leadership talents are and where they are not. In the most severe cases of level three accusations, for example child molestation, it would be very wise to call in those with greater legal knowledge than yours if you are limited in this area. There are going to be legal issues that will have to be addressed in a competent way in such circumstances. If the team member is married and has a family, they will need to be ministered to, perhaps even protected during this time, especially in the early hours of discovery.

Remember, an accusation based on suspicion is not the same thing as an accusation based upon hard, incontrovertible evidence. You do not want to bail out on a team member during the most difficult hour of their ministry only to learn that there was no basis in fact whatsoever regarding the accusation. The heart and soul of contemporary gossip involves where a person has been seen and with whom that person was seen. Reputations have been at risk based upon the assumptions of conclusion-jumping individuals. Even the apostle Paul was a target of such an assumption once (see Acts 21:28).

A wise pastor once told me, "Any person is capable of doing anything under the right set of circumstances." While this may be true, when it comes to accusations I reserve the right to evaluate the validity of the witness. When a team member who has been demonstrably faithful, dependable, gifted, called, credible, and worthy of my support falls suspect under an accusation, one of the first things I am going to do is examine the character of the accuser.

There is a scriptural principle regarding this conviction. The first time I read Proverbs 11:11, "By the blessing of the upright the city is exalted: but it is overthrown by the mouth of the wicked," I was convicted about the influence of ungodly leaders. They cannot be trusted. You cannot believe their campaign promises, and you cannot trust them when they claim a desire to have equal rights. In the same way, why in the world should anyone give credibility to the mouth of the wicked when it comes to an accusation about a proven team member?

Remain calm, listen for all the information, critically evaluate the evidence, examine the credibility of the witness, and then determine the most effective strategy for dealing with a level three accusation.

Valid. . . But Not Terminal

An accusation can be valid without being terminal. A team member may be guilty of poor decision-making, conduct inappropriate for a minister, or deficiency in certain ministry skills needed for the work to which they have been called. When these valid accusations are met with a redemptive response, both the church and the minster become winners.

When it is determined that a team member has a valid weakness, the team builder has the opportunity to enable significant life changes and ministry preservation. Let's say that a member of the team is consistently late for appointments, often shows a lack of preparation, and is low in overall ministry effectiveness. There may be a few simple enrichment measures that could be taken to enable this minister to become much more effective in the future. Time-management courses are available from many sources. Skill workshops are structured to provide additional training and motivation for individuals in ministry. Counseling is also available from several qualified sources specializing in ministerial burn-out.

When confronting the team member about the valid accusations, a redemptive and responsible leader will make the completion of any one, if not all, of the available experiences a requirement. During annual evaluations, these areas may be easily identified as expectations for the team member during the following year. When confronting the team member at a mid-point during the year, making completion of such training or enrichment a mandatory stipulation is also very appropriate. Follow-up can be easy to observe and inspect. Over a relatively short time, productivity by this minister should improve, making him more valuable to the team and to the body of the church. Relationships did not have to be severed, and the church did not have to experience the agony of a forced termination.

This illustration seems rather simple. However, the principle is important and should be transferable to almost any situation:

- The value of the team member is increased.
- Inspection ensures accountability.
- Expectations are presented and corrective steps identified.
- Confrontation is made and accepted.
- An accusation is verified and proven to be valid.

When you determine that an accusation is not terminal, you have followed the initial process identified in this chapter of intake, interview, investigation, and instruction. You must now add a fifth ingredient: *inspection.* People do not always do what we expect, but they almost always do what we inspect! Team builders have the right to be inspectors. It is one of the many ways in which we minister and lead.

Terminal Accusations

It is a new day in church history. Never before have law suits been filed against the church as they have in recent years for sexual misconduct or other forms of unethical behavior. Forced terminations among clergy are also at an all-time high, many involving charges stemming from ethical violations. It is imperative that the team builder consider the vast scope of potential ramifications involved when the painful need to terminate a member of the team arises.

Legal ramifications. I am not a skilled communicator in addressing the legal issues regarding employment. You should be familiar with your local state laws in this area prior to making the decision to terminate over accusations that are made against members of your team. In our redemptive role as pastors we try to handle things with integrity while at the same time preserving the reputation of our church. Sometimes, even with noble intentions, we terminate due to the violation of church covenant or unethical behavior and then find ourselves the target of litigation by the former employee. Incident documentation and annual, written, signed evidence that an employee understands all of the expectations may be valuable in the event that terminal issues arise in the church.

Your knowledge of the law becomes crucial in these matters. Anyone willing to violate the higher laws of God is going to find using the legal system to their benefit a snap. In fact, they will find great pleasure in fighting it out in an environment that is foreign and hostile toward the church. Our courtrooms have become such an environment in this century. Don't think for a moment that your situation is different. You are dealing with someone who has already lost their character; what more do they have to lose?

Fellowship ramifications. While you should never let it be a reason for inaction, never underestimate the potential fallout that could occur following the termination of a member of your team. Relationships have been established by this team member over the years they've been in your congregation. Some people look to them as unquestionably fit for ministry. Those who do not know the details may be sympathetic toward the team member, or they may even be deceived by the lies about your character and leadership ability during the terminal investigation. Do not be surprised if people side with these team members and follow them to other churches.

This is why it is important to *be open and honest with your congregation* during times like this. In a generic way, you need to inform the congregation of what has happened, how it was investigated, what options were available and the decision that was made. Times like this are times when the church needs to be in a concert of prayer for all parties involved in the circumstances leading up to termination. *Trying to keep everything a secret will only give an opportunity for the facts to be misconstrued and for the reputation of your church to suffer further damage.* We all know that bad news travels fast.

Spiritual ramifications. When an accusation is valid, quick and decisive action is required. The senior pastor must recognize this as one of leadership's responsibilities. There are spiritual principles involved which will have a long-reaching impact upon the ministry of the church. It becomes a matter of trust. Are you willing to trust God with the potential impact this will have upon the fellowship of the church? If your motives are right and if a team member has fallen, will the cause of Christ be better served by retaining this individual or not?

You may fear the potential loss of members in terminating a popular team member. This potential reality is nothing compared to the judgment of God that may be experienced in failing to lead in times like this. God's judgment may be manifested in the absence of His presence and the absence of His blessing in your ministry. Allowing the team member to stay may prevent a church exodus, but don't expect God's presence to remain. In tolerating sin, we inoculate our church with a vaccine making them immune to any possible further conviction over sin. The end results are devastating. You can fight in the flesh for a time, but eventually, you will learn that you are no match for the spiritual adversary of ours souls without the blessing of the Father.

What Are Terminal Accusations?

Terminal accusations are those things that necessitate a severance of an individual's membership on the team. For most of us, any proven accusation dealing with sexual misconduct must be dealt with through termination for the church to have credibility in the future. We may not terminate the membership of a layperson who comes and confesses sexual sin, but when it comes to the pastoral team, there is a higher standard (not a double standard) of expectation that must be honored.

When sexual misconduct is verified, termination should be immediate. This can be done discretely, but in most cases, the secret will travel faster than any other news-worthy topic from the church. It is best to admit it, share the generic details with the church in an open meeting, ask God for grace in the situation, and move on.

If a staff member has fallen into a pattern of sin that disqualifies them from spiritual leadership, there may be ways for the church to act redemptively, but this does not mean that the individual remains in an area of spiritual leadership. There may be a desire on the part of the church to minister to the family by providing resources for their immediate needs. This is gracious. Furthermore, some will want to see that the minister receives counseling, therapy, even legal assistance. At any rate, the leader of the team must act with integrity and clarity of vision to see that the ministry of the church and the name of Jesus Christ are not further damaged in the community by tolerating or ignoring immoral behavior among the leadership of the church.

In some cases a minister can be restored to a place of spiritual leadership following an act or even a brief season of immorality. However, there must be incontrovertible evidence of the following:

- Admission of responsibility
- Complete repentance
- Brokenness
- Appropriate counseling
- Restitution
- Accountability

Without any one of these elements, it is doubtful that genuine change has taken place. In most cases, a tremendous investment has been made in the academic preparation of team members, not to mention the mentoring and discipling that have been given to them over the years. While not excusing poor decisions, we need to understand that the failure may have come at a time when personal crises were taking an inestimable toll on the minister. A temporary mental illness could have been a real factor. There may have been a number of other personal issues present that were simply met with the wrong response from this minister. In cases like this, we can afford to be redemptive.

In other situations, there is evidence that the failure has been a part of an ongoing, habitual pattern in the life of this individual. Worse, there is no evidence of repentance or brokenness. It becomes a point of grace, not to mention leadership, that appropriate discipline be exercised firmly, quickly, and completely. Other terminal issues may involve any combination of team disloyalty, a severe breech of church covenant, compulsive behavior disorders, or even persistent laziness. What you have to remember in facing these situations is that you are dealing with individuals who have deliberately chosen to remove themselves from the team already. You simply are bringing formal closure to the relationship.

Epilogue

Team building brings multiple, long-term benefits. The *senior leader* benefits by multiplying his ministry and forging significant relationships that will impact the Kingdom of God for years. *Team members* benefit because they have the opportunity of growing and maturing in a nurturing environment. Theirs truly is a Paul/Timothy relationship. The *congregation* benefits by being blessed with growing leaders. Instead of constantly replacing staff vacancies every 18 months, congregations led by team-building pastors enjoy longer pastoral tenures from every member of the pastoral team and can focus energy and resources on the mission of the church. The *community* stands to receive a blessing because the spiritual leaders in the church are living a life that exemplifies and models the best of Christian leadership.

Team building is a process whereby a senior leader invests himself into the lives of others to effect a stronger, broader, longer-lasting ministry. The team builder sees immediate results in the present ministry setting and will look back over the years to see multiplied congregations being served and equipped by team builders. Team building can be contagious, but it requires vision and discipline.

Looking at today's horizon, it could be how the leaders of winning churches will relate to one another and organize for ministry. The passion for team building is born out of a conviction that the best days for ministry are not in the past but in the future. There has not been a greater opportunity for communicating the gospel in the history of mankind. If we fail to experience a great awakening in the coming 10 years, it will be the greatest spiritual failure of all mankind.

Team building could be the answer to the disturbing trend of escalating forced terminations, restlessness among professional clergy, dissatisfaction experienced by the spouses, and dysfunctional relationships in the family of faith brought on by hostility and adversarial positioning exhibited within existing "staff" structures.

Finally, team building is not so much something you do, it is something that grows out of who you are in Christ. It begins with your relationship with God, who called you to experience His grace, and it is only His grace that enables you to build winning teams in every arena into which He calls you.

Let's build the greatest teams our world has ever seen!